Bruce MacDougall is the Executive Secretary of Hamilton Conference. He is an enthusiastic, but not very good tennis player, a Conference planner, writer, father, photographer, grandfather and plays 1940's music on the piano, but not very well. His past includes tours of duty as a chauffeur, a time in the Canadian Navy, lawyer, parish minister, religious radio host (he couldn't make up his mind what he wanted to be when he grew up!) and founder of Telecare, the first telephone crisis ministry in Canada using trained lay people and now part of a world-wide network. Prior to coming to Hamilton Conference in 1985, he was President of Faith at Work, USA, residing in Columbia, Maryland, and before that, Director of Faith at Work, Canada. This is his third book. His previous two were not in the top ten best sellers. In 1982, he was awarded an honourary DD by Huntington University, Sudbury. He is married to the former Isobel McDougall. They have five children and three grandchildren. Although born and raised in Edmonton, he is a graduate of Carleton University, Ottawa, Osgoode Law School, Toronto and Emmanuel College, Victoria University.

*This book could not have been produced without the patient help of Alicia Haynes.*

A Time to Travel Light

# A Time to Travel Light

### By Bruce MacDougall

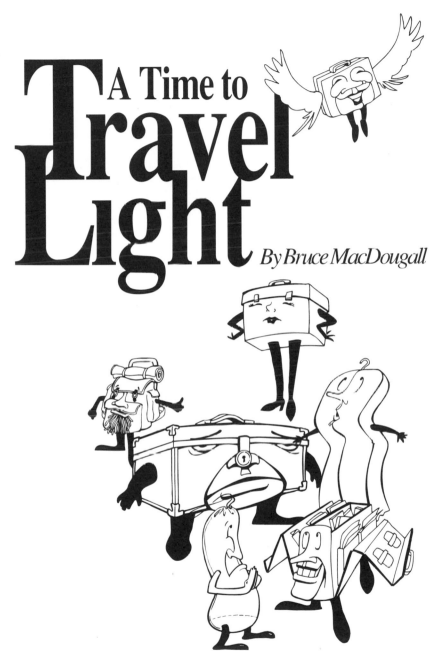

THE UNITED CHURCH PUBLISHING HOUSE

ISBN – 0-919000-69-X

Publisher: R.L. Naylor
Editor-in-Chief: Peter Gordon White
Editorial Assistant: Elizabeth Phinney
Book Design: Tunley Maynard Design Associates
Printing: Ainsworth Press

**Canadian Cataloguing in Publication Data**
MacDougall, Bruce, 1925-
    A time to travel light

ISBN 0-919000-68-X

1. Christian life – 1960-   . I. Title
BV4501.2.M23 1990 248.2 C90-093852-8
890432

# Introduction

Many of us Christians carry a lot of "baggage," laid on us by the church and ourselves. Most of it has nothing to do with the faith.

It's time to let it go!

This book names some of my "baggage pieces." You have your own.

To help you find out whether my list is yours, too, there are three questions at the end of each chapter. I invite you to answer them if you care about yourself and the church.

— Bruce MacDougall

# Baggage List

## Chapter 1

*The Steamer Trunk*

# The Boredom of Sunday Worship

I t is Thursday evening and the minister meets with a worship committee (which changes every six to eight weeks) to plan the Sunday service. The worship is very Presbyterian/Methodist/United Church-ish. It follows the lectionary passages, so the committee reads the scripture and the commentary and questions which the minister provides in the monthly lectionary. They talk about the scripture. What does it mean? Does anybody identify with the passage? They talk about the prayers, hymns, special announcements. Then comes the question of who will take what parts of the service and particularly how they will deal with that part of the service that comes under the heading of sermon, since the minister doesn't preach. In fact, he really doesn't take part in the service except after the "message" time, when he may help to bring more focus to the "message" or solicit comments from the table groups.

On Sunday, the congregation gathers in the upstairs of an old building that was once a carriage house. It is very comfortable. The floor has been carpeted and a huge stone fireplace dominates one wall. The "worship centre" consists of a lectern and an old bar stool in front of the fireplace. Banners, made at congregational retreats, hang from the ceiling. There is a shaft of light from the cupola in the centre of the roof that looks like, and feels like, a symbol of God's presence. As people enter, they pick up a coffee, proceed upstairs and sit down at one of the tables set for eight.

The music is taped because they don't have an organ or an organist. The service begins, each part taken by some member of the committee. When it comes to "sermon" time, one member of the committee may tell what the passage means to them or how it impinges on their life or there may be a dialogue about the passage or they may use clowns, or any other imaginative way in order to get the point of the lesson across. Then the congregation are given a couple of questions to help them to get into the scripture and discover what it means for them personally, for the community or for the world. The table groups are informal. There are no leaders. People share or not as they feel comfortable. Finally, after about 20 minutes, a member of the committee or the minister may invite comments or questions from the groups.

Of course this brief description does not do justice to the process, because the impact of such worship cannot be measured in one service. It is the conduct of worship like this, week in and week out, year in and year out, from which a tremendous sense of community arises. The music chosen, the prayers spoken and requested, are based on a real knowledge of the congregation. The sharing of the worship committee members and at the table groups, provides a quality of real life that is exciting, scary, and full of integrity. Finally, I should say that you might not like this kind of worship. It certainly is no panacea. But the one thing that I can guarantee is that you would never be bored.

This is fact, not fantasy. It is real. It is the way the Kittamaqundi Community Church in Columbia, Maryland, worships each Sunday. I attended that church for five and a half years, from 1980 to 1985. This small congregation of approximately 120 persons is a spin-off from the Church of the Saviour in Washington, DC. Its Enabling Minister, Gerry Goethe, is an ordained minister with the United Methodist Church. The congregation is made up of disenchanted Presbyterians, Baptists, Episcopalians, Methodists, Roman Catholics and agnostics, most of whom are divorced, divorcing, separated, or separating. They are very much like any other congregation except that they are very open about their pain and their brokenness and their needs.

Besides the true-to-life quality of the worship service and its unconfutable reality, it is a tremendous affirmation of the members of the congregation. But it is not easily attained. In the first two years that I attended, I could hardly stand to listen to lay people stumble and fumble and bumble along. I kept hoping that the minister would take over and give the service a little class. But he refused. He kept on encouraging, affirming, assuring, until they got past trying to imitate the minister and began to believe him when he told them that they were a gifted people. Now don't misunderstand. These lay people did not start producing perfect Sunday worship. They bombed, in about the same ratio, as we clergy do. Nor was the congregational life idyllic. Because people are people, it had the same kinds of struggles as any congregation. But their model for congregational life was full of hope.

Contrast that service, which in itself is a celebration of and by the people, with the average service of public worship in the average main-line church today, which is so clergy dominated and, weekly, boring. I don't mean that the men and women who lead the worship are themselves boring, but rather that the worship process is. As a former professor of public worship at Emmanuel College once said, "A United Church service of worship tends to be a monologue by the minister broken only by the congregation or choir bursting into song when the minister has stopped."

I believe that most of us clergy lead public worship the way we do because we were taught to do it that way in seminary, by those we believed were experts. After all, they were professors weren't they? My guess is that most of us in the order of ministry discovered within the first few years that seminary-taught worship may not be the end-all after all. The result is a little cosmetic innovation here and there. The laity are invited to welcome the congregation, to do the call to worship, to read the lessons, and to make announcements. Sometimes selected people are invited to help the minister prepare the sermon.

In order to survive the worship service on Sunday, some clergy form lectionary groups. The lectionary groups are a marvellous idea. We clergy need all the encouragement we can get to meet the expectations of the weekly service of worship. I can also see the lectionary groups for clergy as a group meeting out of desperation, because it is so unrealistic that one person can provide a relevant, life-touching message every week. I suppose that's why so many sermons are filled with illustrations from books and why some clergy listen to every conversation with a view to picking up an exciting illustration for next week's sermon. We clergy do that in spite of the fact that our congregations are filled with hundreds of real-life stories, if we would only give our people permission to contribute to the Sunday service. Just think of the credibility factor that could be added to the Sunday service, if the preacher would illustrate his/her point with the life experiences of members of the congregation.

In the report entitled *Project Ministry Revisited*, by Dr. Anne Squire, it is stated that as the church becomes visible in its gatherings as the Body of Christ there are fundamental elements or marks of the church. One of those marks is the telling of the story. But the important point is that the telling of the story should not be confined to the clergy.

For 15 years I worked for a para-church ministry called Faith at Work. Its goal was the equipping and the enabling of the laity in the churches. We often started our group processes with some giving of history. Some people were not comfortable with that. They felt we should be starting with the Bible or with theology. Some felt that history giving was merely a psychological gimmick and not very Christian. Some theologians considered it to be mere subjectivism. But the fact is that our own honest theology is unfolding in our own personal history. It is true to say "my God is to be found in my story."

Stan Jones, a Presbyterian minister from California with whom I worked in Faith at Work, has been very helpful to me in this matter of story-telling. He reminds me of the difference between the people of Israel and other nations in their searching after God. In the early chapters of the Old Testament, we are told of nations who built a tower to find God, but the Hebrew people had a different understanding. They had experienced God breaking into their history and they expected more. So they were called sojourners and venturers who journeyed toward the Promised Land expecting God to break into the ordinary events of their lives.

Greek-thinking persons sought God among the deities of Mount Olympus. The animist looked for gods in the unusual and powerful events of nature. And if you were an astrologer you looked to the stars for clues about God.

But the people of Israel sought their God in human history. That's why, if you asked a Hebrew to tell you about their God, he or she would say, "My father was a wandering Aramean who went down to Egypt and there fell into slavery. And Jahweh brought us out of Egypt...."

But wait, says the Greek-thinking person, I asked you about God, not about your history, to which the Hebrew would reply, "I cannot tell you about God without telling you about my history." The Hebraic-Christian biblical language is not as we know it ontological, metaphysical or mystical. It is always historical. Thus telling the story is the most legitimate form of theological conversation.

However, there is another story for those of us who have prepared ourselves professionally for the ministry. We studied a system of theology that was very important. But most of us did not recognize that a very crucial experiential theology was unfolding in the midst of our marriages, or with our children or with our struggle with our own selfhood.

It is not that God is confined to our histories. The scriptures are the whole story of God, but what we experience of God shows up in our history. No matter what is said to you conceptually about God, you will see the God that we really know and trust in our history. Here our true theology is unfolding.

William Barclay quotes an eminent British preacher as once saying that there are not four gospels, but five. There is Matthew, Mark, Luke and John and our own personal story. And this man says the most important of the five is the fifth gospel.

Now of course I realize that involving the laity of our church in the sharing of their story isn't going to happen overnight. After all we have been telling the members of our congregation for the past 2,000 years that they are sheep, empty vessels, and theologically inept, so that by now their sense of inadequacy is in the genes. But it is reversible and it depends upon us clergy accepting a new role as enablers of a body of gifted men and women, as those who call forth the gifts of our brothers and sisters. It is no coincidence that some of the synonyms for *enable* are "confer," "empower," "invest," and "strengthen." That is our new role.

You can see why the present service of worship on Sunday is so unreal and boring. We clergy are trying desperately to make the service of worship relevant and helpful. We are trying to be creative and imaginative. But it is all a guessing game. It is ecclesiastical roulette. It's really a weekly lottery because we don't know what the needs are of most of the congregation. Many of us clergy are not sensitive to the boredom factor because we enjoy leading the service. The only time I am not bored in a traditional service is when I am preaching. But that can also make me rather numb to the needs of the congregation.

Most congregational life today is based on the principle that everything is okay. Isn't that the conclusion to be drawn? I've never heard anyone in an ordinary congregation get up in a Sunday service of worship and share something of the struggle or pain in their lives. On the contrary, we are not encouraged to be open or vulnerable. At a recent anniversary service, when I asked for congregational participation during the "sermon," a man stood up and said that "The church must be a place of holiness, purity and cleanliness." My guess is that his view is shared by many. But who could be open in that kind of environment?

And we clergy are caught up in the same dynamics. We seldom feel free to share our struggle or our pain with the congregation. The same professor of worship at Emmanuel told us, "Gentlemen (there were no women), present your conclusions and not your doubts." It took me close to 15 years to wake up to the fact that what he was really saying was, "Don't be open, don't share your struggle. Be confident, have the answers, etc., etc." So if the clergy are not free to share their needs and the congregation is playing the same game, how can the service of worship express any reality?

It struck me the other day in church that our attitude of non-risk and non-openness or vulnerability, which are contributors to the boredom factor, is expressed in large measure by the way we dress when we go to church. Our clothes, for many, are a theological statement of where we are. In the congregation of which I spoke in Columbia, Maryland, people came to church in almost anything: suits, jackets, jeans, cut-offs, shirt and tie, shirt and no tie, shoes, no shoes. Their clothing was a symbol of the openness and vulnerability of those people who came to church to seek the reality of God for their broken, hurting, shattered lives because, as I have said, most of them were coming out of broken relationships.

In contrast, the church I attend in Hamilton isn't quite striped trousers and cut-away coats, but it is a dark blue pin-striped congregation. It occurred to me last winter that if I were to stand in the centre aisle in my three piece blue pinstripe suit and ask people for words to describe what they saw, my guess is that they would use words like neat, tidy, clean-cut, successful, confident, reliable, in charge, in control. And I wondered to myself how I could really come to confess my sin, pray for forgiveness, seek help, when everything about me oozes control and denies any need of these things. So again, if I come to church and my dress reflects an attitude of self-sufficiency, then I will be bored because a service which speaks of sin and forgiveness will not speak to me where I am. I don't need God. I need some confirmation that my sense of self-sufficiency and control are what is required.

Most of those who give leadership in worship are so burdened down with the ecclesiastical hardware of stoles, gowns, hoods, tabs, etc., that they hardly model the picture of the penitent person. I don't know about you, but when I look at the average clergyperson in charge of the service, I say to myself, he/she must have everything in control. They are in charge. The gowns and the assorted stoles speak of authority, of office, of position, and of power. They prepare these beautiful orders of service. They are often masterful. They are usually orchestrated to the very closing second, so that the television hour will not be offended. Everything flows right. The sequence of ingredients is theologically and psychologically sound. But it is still an orchestrated guess. And the gifted people with so much to contribute sit there like sheep bored to death. And we clergy, though perhaps not bored, are frustrated. And if the congregations are not bored, it's because they have become spiritually and psychologically comatose.

My guess is that some brother and sister clergy might feel a tad upset by my comments. But please don't be. I am part of the problem too and have been for thirty years. I'm not advocating that we get rid of theologically trained leaders. The church needs trained persons. What needs to be changed is the role of the clergy and the function of the clergy. Preparing a Sunday service and visiting the sick is peanuts compared to the task of helping the laity discover, claim, and use their giftedness to share the reality of their lives with one another. This would be an exercise of real power. To affirm and to help release the giftedness of the people, to be the resource person in the building of the Body of Christ is an opportunity filled with so many possibilities for clergy fulfillment that it defies the imagination. But it will also require a different kind of clergyperson and laity.

The United Church of Canada dealt with this matter at its General Council in 1977. It was a very encouraging report. As a matter of fact, I was downright excited when I read it. Here are some selected statements:

"The good health and perhaps survival of the church depends on whether or not it can hold up a new vision to its people: a vision of a church wherein every person who has acknowledged the claim of Jesus Christ on his or her life has a ministry to perform."

"If this vision is to have a reality, laity must come to realize the truth of the statement, 'We are the church.'"

"Lay persons must actively resist being pressured into pre-determined roles in the congregation which are counter-productive."

"The church must harness the talents of its laity and change the job expectations of its pastors so that a wealth of creative resources is made easily available to those engaged in Christian nurture. The church will die if it is left to the clergy to fulfil the ministry of Jesus. The laity have a role in ministry which is not possible to the ordained; just as the ordained have a necessary ministry which is different from that of the laity. Both must fulfil their ministries if the church of tomorrow is to be faithful to its high calling."

However, if tomorrow every clergyperson in the United Church were to declare that they were going to be enablers of their people from this moment on, nothing would change. Nothing will change until the laity of the church take seriously who and what they are and begin to claim their place in the Body. Then Sunday at eleven o'clock would cease to be boring.

I heard Jesse Jackson speak to some high-school kids about drugs. He said to them "I am here because I care about you and your problems, but you must never allow anyone to care more about you and your problems than you care about yourself and your problems. Otherwise nothing will ever happen." What is true for those youngsters is also true for the laity of the church today. The laity are no longer a collection of empty vessels who have come on Sunday to be filled by the clergy.

There was a time, perhaps, when the symbolism of the worship area was appropriate. That is, the sanctuary was in the form of a cross and the services were led from the chancel. Or it may be quite true that the centre pulpit was appropriate after the Reformation. But today, we need a new place of worship which bears witness to our claimed belief of the priesthood of all believers. We need some inspired architects who have a new vision of how a sanctuary can symbolize the new place of laity and clergy. One thing is for sure; the pews must go and be replaced with comfortable moveable chairs that can be set row on row, or in a circle, or in groups, or however, according to the demands of the lesson, the leading of the Spirit, and the needs of the congregation. We cannot go on seating people in rows to look at the back of each other's heads and watch the performance that is being performed on the chancel.

In my position I do a considerable amount of anniversary preaching and it is an unnerving experience to go into most of the congregations and discover that the people there are my age (early to mid-sixties) or older. We must act soon or we will not only be confronted by empty vessels, but with empty pews.

Another reason for the boredom factor is that we are doing things in public worship that are appropriate to a community of believers, but the average congregation is not a "community." So the action and reality don't match. We have the words, but not the music. What are the qualities of community? Well, here are some: a common purpose, a common goal, a knowledge of and caring for one another, a trusting of one another, a vulnerability, an openness, a sense of belonging to each other, a sense of responsibility for each other and the common cause, liking to be with one another, and commitment to each other and the purpose.

That is not a description of most of the churches I have attended or pastored. A more accurate list of common factors would be: mortgages, habit, status, a large dose of apathy, lethargy, fear, and self-righteousness.

Robert Raines, in his book, *New Life in the Church*, quotes a German theologian who said, "In Luther's day, people were looking for a gracious God, but today people are looking for a gracious neighbour." That view is supported by Bishop Wilke in his book, *Are We Yet Alive*, at a time when his congregation was failing badly. They tried every known plan to increase the congregation, but nothing worked. The model for increasing membership was to call people to a commitment to Christ and then seek to assimilate them in the congregation. Wilke then discovered that a more appropriate model was to be found in Acts 2:42, 46 and 47. The laity in the church began to bring in newcomers, who before making any commitments, became involved in the life of the church, and those who discovered a community and a gracious neighbour, then made their commitment.

That was precisely the process at the church in Columbia which I attended. No one had made any attempt to get me to join the church after I had attended for several weeks and I must admit that I was a little miffed. But they did invite me to be a part of the Worship Committee, to help with the Old Testament Class and to plan the congregational retreat. It was because of the reality of the community that I knew these were my kind of people. If one decided to become a member of this congregation, he or she was invited to become an intern and to a greater participation in the life of the congregation by taking five or six courses in New Testament, Old Testament, Ethics, etc. One was expected to become a member of a weekly mission group and tithe their gross income.

It was out of that significant participation in the life of the congregation that people made their public profession of faith and became members of the community. The most exciting services were when someone would tell the congregation why they wanted to become a member and in so doing, shared their story. That was not boring. It was a privilege.

Of course we can't do all of that in the average main-line church. After all, people joined the church under quite different rules. We can't suddenly change the rules — or can we? If the situation is serious enough we can do anything.

The Presbyterian Church in Canada was shaken when it read in Reginald Bibby's book, *Fragmented Gods*, that they were a dying church and would not exist in a few more years. They are now in the process of planning some radical changes. The fact is that we in the United Church are in the same position. It's true we have a few more members but that which is destroying our Presbyterian brothers and sisters is also in the bloodstream of the United Church and other main-line denominations. We can change. We can do something radical if the United Church wants to live badly enough. We can do it, not just to save the denomination, but to create the kind of community and fellowship that we deeply desire to be. It will be a fellowship of the people, enabled and loved by well-equipped leaders and our Sunday worship will reflect the new reality that is ours. But there is so much baggage to drop.

---

**Your immediate gut-level reaction to this chapter.**

**Your reflected response after two or three days.**

**Any differences between your reaction and reflection? Is there anything you need to do?**

## Chapter 2

*The Duffle Bag*

# The Illusion of Biblical Authority

T he authority and interpretation of scripture has become an urgent issue for The United Church of Canada and for most other churches. But first, I want to suggest to you that there is a more urgent issue to be faced and that is the illusion of biblical authority. In other words, practically speaking, the Bible is not authoritative for most of us in all of the churches today. And unless we deal with that reality, we will never come to a meaningful understanding of the scripture in our lives.

I realize that not many would agree with that rather provocative statement, so I'll back off a little. The Bible is authoritative to the extent that we are able to find a verse or passage that agrees with our culturally determined point of view. In other words, we, the believers, give the Bible whatever authority it may have for us. Is that better?

Martin Luther in particular would not like that. Luther tried to bring object and subject into relationship. According to editor J. Leslie Dunstan in the book, *Protestantism*, Luther did not believe that authority resided in the object (Bible) with the subject (reader) obliged to play a passive role. Nor does the authority reside in the person, so that the Bible becomes what each individual makes it. The object and subject must be held together, according to Luther. This coming together must take place in the silence of the individual before the Word. It is the waiting of the believer before God that is crucial. Luther thus propounds a new conception of authority. In the last resort, the authority of scripture is not its own possession, held by independent right. For Luther, the scripture is not the Word, but witness to the Word.

I want to suggest that the reality of today is that we have moved beyond the position of Luther. We no longer stand in silence before God (if we ever did) in order to bring object and subject into relation. The subject (person) today is so culturally shaped, that he/she brings his/her position to the object (scripture), but only to find a portion of the object that agrees with or confirms his/her culturally determined position and then it becomes "authority" of a kind.

Of course this suggestion is not new. Dr. James Barr, in his book, *Holy Scripture*, makes it clear that in many cases, it is not the authority of scripture that is primary, but the particular doctrine or denominational position. The Bible is merely used as a prop to support the real authority which is conservatism or Calvinism or liberalism or fundamentalism.

History has made it clear that if the Bible is taken for what it actually says, it could support a great many different theological positions. If the Roman Catholics found their position proved by scripture, so did the Lutherans and the Presbyterians and the Methodists and all other denominations.

Another example of picking and choosing your scripture is to be found in the doctrines of the Virgin Birth, predestination and the inspiration of scriptures, which have little biblical support.

It is also true that certain denominations have a hierarchy of scripture. For example, the Lutherans stress upon the letters of Paul, while the books like James, Hebrews and Revelation are little regarded. Anglicans sit for the Old Testament lesson, but stand for the Gospel.

There is no shortage of examples of this selective authority today. The recent controversy over the possible ordination of practicing homosexuals is a contemporary and clear illustration of how much the subject determines what authority the object will have. In my position as a conference secretary, I attended a number of congregational, presbytery, conference, and General Council meetings where the issue was debated. Invariably, the debaters from all sides would quote some passage of scripture to support their position. Members of the Community of Concern and others opposed to the ordination of practicing homosexuals, would quote passages from Leviticus and Romans. Their position was clear. The Bible was against homosexuality and therefore the proposal to ordain self-declared practicing homosexuals must be stopped. But for one who wanted to take the Bible seriously, it was a very confusing experience. Let me explain.

Those persons in opposition argued that Leviticus spoke clearly against homosexuality. They cited Leviticus 20:13 and 22. And they were right. Leviticus is definitely not in favour of homosexuality. "If a man has intercourse with a man as with a woman, they both commit an abomination.

They shall be put to death." That is pretty clear! But the question is, why are they are so selective? Why don't they take seriously the remainder of Chapter 20, where a man who has sex with a woman and her mother shall be burned or if a man has intercourse during the menstrual period, they shall be cut off from the people, etc.?

In the very next chapter, it is made clear that certain men are not acceptable for the priesthood. Men who have a physical defect or handicap may not approach to offer the bread to God. The blind, the lame, the hunchback and dwarf; none of these are acceptable according to the scriptures. But we never hear anyone these days calling for the dismissal of clergypersons because of a physical handicap. So why is it that only one verse of the two chapters of Leviticus that deal with homosexuality is pulled out and held up to be the Word of God?

One of the most obvious indifferences to the scriptures is to be found in Matthew 25 where Jesus refers to the needs of the hungry, the thirsty, the stranger and the sick, etc. In 1985-86, millions of men, women and children died in Ethiopia from starvation. The Hamilton Conference Office of the United Church did not receive a single letter or petition expressing outrage that the United Church was generally indifferent to the deaths of these people. Now, five years later, we are being warned that in this next year the Ethiopians will once again need our help or thousands will die of starvation.

There are, as we all know, a lot of other verses in the Bible that we disregard today, both in the liberal and conservative churches. Many of them refer to women. Paul makes it clear in 1 Timothy that women must dress modestly and with no elaborate hair style and not be decked out with jewels or expensive clothes, but we don't pay attention to that any more. Have you seen a Pentecostal choir lately? Paul says that women must be learners and listen quietly with due submission, but we don't pay any attention to that either, otherwise there wouldn't be any churches today. We are also told that a woman yielded to temptation in the Garden of Eden, but she will be saved by motherhood. Do we buy that today? I guess not! Paul also says that if a man can't control his own family, he isn't fit to control a congregation. That too seems to have slipped by. So how is it that we are so selective, if the Bible is the Word of God and we are under its authority?

St. Paul is clear that Christians should settle their problems and keep out of the civil courts. It is obvious that we do not obey that. And we never have. You should read the story of the origins of the United Church where the legal battles continued for some 14 years after union. The dissenting Calvinists thought that the law was the only way to deal with the lower nature of man. (And "man," in that case, referred to the males who entered the union.)

During the past year, when some congregations decided to leave the United Church, they wanted to take their property despite the fact that they and their ministers knew that all property is held by local trustees, in trust, for The United Church of Canada. But the Community of Concern said it would support class actions against the United Church for property. When I asked a member of the Community of Concern executive how he could do that in light of the scripture, he said it was true that "We should not take the initiative and sue"; but, (there is always a 'but') "while we should not take the initiative in the Courts, when it comes to defending our own property, that is different."

Jesus made it clear that divorce is bad news and wrong, but we are not guided by that view any more. For a long time the United Church clergy played a game of marrying "delinquent" Anglicans, but times have changed and the Anglicans have now arranged to marry their own. The Romans wouldn't marry divorced persons. They played the game of "annulment."

Now the citing of the above is not to put down certain Christians, but simply to make the point of the myth of biblical authority whether we look at the Bible individually or corporately. It is a very selective process. And what is true of conservative Christians is equally true on the liberal side. They too choose verses which support their views and ignore those with which they disagree. The bottom line is that today the subject (people) give the object (the Bible) its authority. I'm not suggesting that this is right, but then it may be. John Calvin said that the Bible "never seriously affects us 'til it is confirmed by the spirit in our hearts." That's getting pretty close.

Lest I be accused of blaming others for the sins of which I am also guilty, let me say that my own personal experience confirms all that I have suggested. Today I have a "Three S" approach to biblical authority which is the methodology of most Christians. It is selective, subjective and slippery and I shall explain its workings.

Faith at Work, a para-ministry for which I worked for some 13 years, was a first cousin of AA (Alcoholics Anonymous). So the ministry of Faith at Work was that of encouraging people to be open and vulnerable and honest about who and what they were, supported by a caring community of faith, because we believed that that was the way to experience the reality of God in our lives.

That was a radical change of thinking for me, but it was so meaningful, that guess what Bible verse became authority for me and became a favourite verse? I'll tell you. 2 Corinthians 12:9, which records a conversation between Paul and God.

God says, "My grace is sufficient for you, for my power is made perfect in weakness."

To which Paul replies, "I will all the more gladly boast of my weaknesses, that the power of Christ may rest upon me, because when I am weak then I am strong."

That verse fitted me exactly where I was and so it became authoritative in my life. But it was very subjective and very selective.

Over the years, I came to have such a high regard for the laity and clergy people who I was meeting in my work, that what St. Paul said about his friends in Philippians 1 became another favourite and authoritative verse for me and my life. It is the first few verses of Philippians 1, especially paraphrased by Leslie Brandt. This is what Paul says about the people with whom he worked:

*"I have met some beautiful people*
*in the course of my travels.*
*They are my sisters and brothers in Christ,*
*fellow servants in the Kingdom work of God.*
*Every time I think about them, I do so prayerfully and a surge of joy fills my heart."*

Once when I was getting very anxious and uptight about my work, a friend sent me a board on which he had burned the words "Philippians 4:6" and it was signed "Love, Paul." Remember? That verse goes like this: "Have no anxiety about anything, but in everything by prayer and supplication, with thanksgiving, let your request be made known to God and the peace of God which passes all understanding will keep your hearts and minds in Christ Jesus."

That passage spoke to me where I was at that time. The Spirit confirmed it in my heart and it became authoritative for me. As John Calvin would say, it seriously affected my life, because I believe it was confirmed by the Holy Spirit. Just one more. In my declining years, I need to hear the words of Romans 8:38 and 39:

*"For I am assured that neither death nor life,*
*nor angels, nor principalities,*
*nor things present, nor things to come,*
*nor powers, nor height, nor depth,*
*nor anything in all creation, will be*
*able to separate us from the love of*
*God in Christ Jesus our Lord."*

Those words of Paul speak to me where I am today. I hear them and I listen. These verses helped me to hear the voice of God because they were speaking to me in my condition and in my circumstance. So at a moment in time when my needs and certain words from the scripture intersect, I then am able to declare them to be authoritative for my life.

That kind of biblical authority is real and personal, but it is very subjective. That is not the kind of personal authority which the United Church claims to believe. Did you know that the United Church in its statement of faith says that the Bible contains the only infallible rule of life and faith? Now that is a wonderfully strong, confidence-building statement. The only trouble is we don't believe it. No, you don't! And neither do I!

I'd like to say it is true, but it simply isn't. Think about it for a moment.

Where do you and I look for directions for our life and the decisions of life? I have not known any person in the past five years who has looked to the Bible when making serious decisions about life's vocations, incurring of debt, the spending of money, the stress in personal relations, the purchase of houses, the raising of kids, etc. If it is true that the Bible is the only infallible rule of faith and life, wouldn't we consult the scriptures when making the most important decisions of our lives? Wouldn't we insist that our children consult the Bible in making the many important decisions in *their* lives?

But we don't, because we don't believe it. During the past five years, I have quit one job and taken another. I have built a cottage and bought a house. I have purchased a car and oh yes, after almost 50 years of abstinence from alcoholic beverages, I have started to drink some wine with my meals from time to time and to take a sherry occasionally. I also have to admit that I am no longer tithing as I once tried to do. In none of these situations did I intentionally look first at the only infallible word of faith and life in order to make these decisions. None of these decisions, I suggest, were a clear demonstration of the authority of scripture in my life.

Today we need an opportunity to break some fresh ground in the matter of authority. That opportunity was given by the clear call of the 32nd General Council of the United Church for the study of the authority and interpretation of scripture. Here was our chance. On October 10, 1989, the Theology and Faith Committee, which had been charged with the responsibility of preparing the study process, issued its report and said, "there is no question of whether the Bible has authority for us. It has."

I guess it was too much to expect the Committee to address the prior and embarrassing question of the illusion of biblical authority. Instead of challenging our pragmatic, individual, and culturally-shaped view of biblical authority, and helping us to see that the Bible is really of little authority, the members of the Committee told us what "could be." What we needed was a clear statement of "what is."

However, the members were not insensitive to the question of "what is." One member said, "The Committee is in a sense testing the waters. The study process will help determine whether the Committee's understanding of where the United Church is at in terms of the authority and interpretation of scipture is really where the rest of the church sees itself." Surely all the members of the Committee needed to do was examine their own daily lives and they would begin to get suspicious about whether the Bible was really authoritative. And if that were not enough, they could have spoken to the dozens of liberal and conservative Christians I have spoken to in the past six months who admitted that the illusion of biblical authority is for real. But instead, they said what encouraged us to go on living in the fantasy land of "What Could Be."

Of course, I realize that I am, as people are prone to do, projecting my experiences onto others, but I do it because of my observations and conversations with others. So let us be honest with ourselves. Let us confront the issue that our lives do not clearly demonstrate the authority of scriptures. Perhaps we could then see the need to repent and see the question of interpretation and authority in a different light.

---

**Your immediate gut-level reaction to this chapter.**

**Your reflected response after two or three days.**

**Any differences between your reaction and reflection? Is there anything you need to do?**

## Chapter 3

*The Backpack*

# The Fairy Tale that God has a Plan for your Life

J ust think about it for a moment. God has a plan for your life!

Taken seriously, it is a very exciting and attractive concept. It is mind-boggling to think that God could have a particular plan and purpose for the four billion men and women on the planet Earth. You think that Cray computers are impressive!

In a sense, such a concept is a necessary corollary to the doctrine of sin. We are sinners and therefore we could not possibly know what it is that God would have us do or be. Hence, God has the plan. The right plan for your life and mine.

We see this divine plan process more clearly in those who are in the professional ordained/commissioned ministry. A section of the Basis of Union of the United Church says that those eligible for the ministry are those who have received a special, individual communication from Jesus, saying, "I am calling you to the ordained/commissioned ministry." He doesn't put it quite that way, but that is the gist of it. If you get that message, you are on your way. If you don't, forget it, because at the ordination/commission service, if you get that far, you will be asked to publicly declare that you have been called by God. In other words, God has revealed to you his particular plan for your life. That's pretty heady stuff. It's the kind of thing we want to believe in. It's very reassuring. Incidentally, that is why, at the Annual Meeting of the Conferences of The United Church of Canada, we only allow those who are being ordained/commissioned to speak about their call to the ministry. You never hear a lay person tell of their call, because if they had one, they wouldn't be a lay person. Lay people are individuals waiting for that special call and if they receive it, they go to be ordained/commissioned. If they don't receive it, they become Elders or Presidents of UCWs.

In general, the process works something like this. Once, a long time ago, I volitionally decided that I wanted to put my life under the management of Jesus Christ, whatever that meant. The next step was to wonder what I should do with my life now that I was a Christian. However, I was told that since I was a sinner, it was not possible for me to know what I should do. Therefore, I was told to pray about it, "Lord, what would you have me do?"

And that was exciting! Any day, maybe today, maybe tomorrow, next week, God would show me, tell me, give me a hint, about what I should be doing with my life. What could be more breathtaking? What greater demonstration of God's love and concern? So I proceeded with great confidence. I asked the Almighty God, the Father of Abraham and Sarah, Isaac and Jacob, the Father of our Lord Jesus Christ, to tell me what to do with my life. I did it believing that God cares what I do. I did it believing that what I might do would make a difference to God and the world. I didn't know how God would communicate the plan to me, but somehow I would find out. I was very fortunate. I had an older friend with whom I shared about 3,000 lunches. He listened, he helped me test the hints, and he encouraged me.

After several years with no clear message having been received, I began to share my anxiety with my friends. They were not very helpful. They told me I wasn't praying enough. They told me I wasn't reading the Bible enough or going to church enough. So now I had two problems, life's direction and devotional failure. Why was God so reluctant to tell me the plan?

About six years later, I became conscious that I felt I should go to theological college and enter the full-time ordained ministry. I felt very good about the idea, but I can also remember feeling very uncomfortable about the idea that God had called me to the ministry. People told me that that was what had happened. The questions asked of me by the church presumed that I was there because I had received that special individual communication from Jesus, "I am calling you to the ordained ministry." What could I say, except that God had certainly been slow in letting me know.

Part of the problem was the fact that I knew a considerable number of older and devoted people who had been praying all their lives for vocational guidance and direction as I had done, but who had never felt they had received any leading or any guidance. The result was a feeling on their part of failure and inadequacy, of not measuring up in some way to what God expected. So it followed that if someone like myself were to declare a sense of clear guidance, then that person must be closer to God, more devoted, more spiritual, more worthy, more everything, which of course was nonsense.

It is also interesting to me how this sense of call by God is so intimidating of those close to you. No one in my close circle of friends dared question "the call." In fact, they hurried to confirm it. On the other hand, when I told my father, he cried. Isobel, my wife, did not argue, even though it meant an enormous change in plans, hopes and lifestyle, because both Isobel and my father felt they could not argue with God. Declaring that you are acting under the direction of God has the wonderful effect of getting everybody in line to support "the call." After all, who wants to be seen opposing the Will of God? Oral Roberts knows this very well.

If it works once, you keep on trying, right? Over the years, I have followed the same process in trying to make important decisions. In retrospect, I can say that I received an answer most quickly to the question of whether or not I should accept a call to a larger church. I don't know why, but the answer seemed to come through unequivocally and rather rapidly. However, I do confess that I was always nervous about the process.

The turning point for me came after a decision I made not to move to the United States. I had really struggled with the decision and when it was over it seemed to me that God had not revealed to me the plan and I was frankly angry. However, after I made my decision, I thought I had received what I would describe as a message from God. (Though I am very nervous in saying that.) This was the message, (right now I'm feeling a little like Isaiah when he said "Thus sayeth the Lord") and it was very clear: "Stop passing the buck to me." I could hardly believe it. But there was more. "Stop passing the buck to me. Make up your own mind about these matters and know that I am with you, whether your decision is right or wrong. But you are responsible." That was both freeing and frightening. It was very affirming and very heavy.

After that experience, I remembered friends of mine who talked about "sanctified common sense" in the decision-making process. It sounded right to me at the time and this "message" of mine seemed to confirm that approach. It also had a lot of implications. It meant that what I wanted to do was not necessarily at odds with God's choice. It meant God was willing to take a chance on my sanctified common sense. It meant that, right or wrong, God was not separated from me. It meant that no decision was forever. It was very liberating.

As a result of that decision, when I was again asked to go to the United States, I didn't pray about it for a minute. I knew what I wanted to do and I said "yes." You see, I had changed the question from "What does God want me to do?" to "What do I want to do?" It is very important to realize that that question, which might sound very self-centered, is asked in the context of being a person of faith, as a member of the Body of Christ and wanting to be God's person.

The decision to go to the United States felt very right. The only problem with it was that if things turned out differently or badly, I could not blame God or anyone else. I had to be responsible for my decision. But I quickly want to re-emphasize that part of the "message" in which God said, "I am with you, whatever you choose." That is very important.

I have a theory about this business of decision-making by Christians which I think is probably also true for non-Christians, whether it is making the decisions called for in daily life or going into the ordered ministry. I believe that in most instances, if not all, people end up doing what they want or need to do. This is premised on the belief that God can and does operate through our needs, gifts, strengths, and weaknesses. I really believe now that I wanted and needed to go into the ministry all the time. But because of this idea that "God has the plan" and that I had to discover it, I went through those years of lunches and six years of asking, "Lord, what do you want me to do?" If someone had said to me that the question should be, "Bruce, what do you want to do with your life?" I might have saved a lot of time and hours of eating.

This business of decision-making is not easy these days. It is no wonder that we want a little divine help, but I have a hunch that if people faced decisions about life by asking, "where is the energy?" they would come to a decision much more quickly. As a matter of fact, I think one could make a case for saying that where the energy is, and where the desire is, is the urging of the Holy Spirit. Let's not fool ourselves, we can never really be one hundred percent sure that we know God's will in these matters, so I say, if there is a chance for error, I would rather err on the side of the energy.

I realize that this is not as exciting a process as the story about being "called" by God. Over the years, I have heard a lot of people, as I am sure you have, talk about their call to the ministry and how they didn't really want to be a minister. They were dragged, kicking and screaming, by God into the ministry. It makes a very good story. Or the other story, which says, "Don't go into the ministry unless it is the last thing you can possibly do." In either case, the message is "Don't do what you might want to do," and "Don't admit to what you want to do." It has so much more authority if we can say "God called me." Well, I say, baloney! It is time we affirmed the power of the Holy Spirit to energize us in the area of our needs and our giftedness, our vocational choices and the decisions we need to make.

Let's go back to the decision sections of the Manual of The United Church of Canada. I want to suggest that the Basis of Union and Section 20 of the Manual dealing with the ministry should be amended to get rid of the pious language in which it is framed. Let us just say that we believe that some people who become Christians experience an inner conviction or call to serve the church and Jesus Christ in the ordained ministry. Then let the church, as it does, provide the means by which that inner leading, that personal need, may be tested. At least, in that way, we are not trying the impossible task of measuring or confirming a call from God.

I guess the problem in part is that people want to believe that the person they set apart for leadership has somehow and someway a more direct connection with God and therefore is better equipped to lead a congregation. But after 65 years of experience, we in the United Church should know how absurd that is. We don't want to believe that the candidate for ministry is in reality fulfilling his/her own needs, which incidentally could be used for the purposes of God.

I want to suggest to you that you not ask God what to do about your life decisions. Rather I want to suggest that you ask yourself, "Where is the energy?" "Where is the interest?" "Where is the excitement?" "Where are my gifts?" "What do I want to do?" And then to see the answers as a way or place of serving God and exercising ministry.

---

**Your immediate gut-level reaction to this chapter.**

**Your reflected response after two or three days.**

**Any differences between your reaction and reflection? Is there anything you need to do?**

## Chapter 4

*The Cosmetic Bag*

# The Fraud of the Victorious Christian Life

I f there was ever an obstacle to be overcome in the Christian race, it is the idea of the victorious Christian life. In a sense, it's like the fairy tale that God has a plan for your life. It is something we want to believe in. It is highly desirable. I suppose that if "victorious" is defined as coping with life, it may be true. However, if it means "controlling" life, if it means avoiding the valleys and leaping from peak to peak, it simply is not true.

The fact is that life is ambiguous, uncertain, perplexing, exciting and joyful. Maybe one can only come to believe that life is ambiguous when one is over the age of 60. Maybe, after all, it's all hormonal. Maybe, that is why, for the first time in my life, I have a poster over my desk which says, "Just when I knew all of life's answers, they changed all the questions." The message of that poster is not, I believe, negative. It is not sounding retreat. It is not a white flag to indicate surrender or mere accommodation to the sometimes overwhelming circumstances of life. It is an invitation to embrace and to engage the uncertainty and ambiguity of life. I could not have put that poster up 20 years ago because I knew both all the answers and all the questions then.

When I lived and worked in the United States, I used to exchange letters with a fellow Christian from Mississippi. He used to write and tell me that the Christian life was a victorious life. If I would only be in the spirit, then life would move from one peak to another. There would be no journeys in the valleys, because Jesus intended for us to be victorious and to enjoy life abundantly.

I now believe that such a view is one which only we middle and upper class Christians could make. It is a culturally determined point of view. We middle class Christians with our success orientation must have a compatible Gospel message and thus the victorious Christian life, because it is a gospel of control. It is an "in-charge" message, in which we are the ones in charge. To admit failure, sin, and the need for forgiveness, simply would not wash.

At the same time, that "victorious" message hooked me, because I remembered that part of the appeal for me, when I decided to put my life under the management of Jesus Christ, was that I would move from a life of ambiguity to one of certainty. That seemed to be very important at the time. The message I picked up from the church and friends and one which is pushed today with great vigor was and is, that to become a Christian is to move from an unsure relationship with God to one of confidence, from aimlessness to one of purposeful living, from restlessness to resolution. It is to move from a certain inner sadness to joy, from the doldrums to a sense of destiny, from unresolved guilt to peace of mind.

Some of the scriptures used to reinforce the "unambiguous quality" of the Christian life were these:
"If anyone is in Christ, he is a new creation, the old has passed away, the new has come."
"Come unto me, and I will give you rest."
"If anyone thirsts, let him come to me and drink."
"I am the bread of life."
"God so loved the world that He gave His only begotten Son."
"So, if the Son makes you free, you shall be free indeed."
"I am the Resurrection and the Life; whoever believes in me shall never die."
"I have come so that you might have life."
"In the world, you have tribulation, but be of good cheer; I have overcome the world."

All of that was and is very appealing to me because it felt like and feels like control. In the early days it felt like God was in control of life and if I belonged to God, I would be in control. Life would not be ambiguous and that was desirable then and now. Later, when I was preaching and counselling men and women to commit themselves to Jesus Christ it was also, I am sure, an invitation for them to move from the uncertainty of life to a sureness and confidence about life because most of them came to me in a moment of real discomfort and one that was very painful.

And there is a certain truth here. When I went to work for Faith at Work in the United States, I went thinking it would be the highlight of my life and career. Within a matter of weeks I discovered I was not the king of the castle, but captain of the Titanic. For the next four years, I presided over the falling and failing of that ministry. During that time, I became very depressed and angry and felt totally out of control.

One Sunday at church I came to the realization that the most important thing in my life was not the success or failure of the ministry, but my relationship to God in Christ. The study was on the Emmaus Road and the leader was saying that whatever else those two people were feeling, they must have been sad, disappointed and perplexed. Then he asked us to be quiet and think about where we were or had been sad, disappointed or perplexed. Then he invited us to share our experiences around the tables of eight. After about 20 minutes, there was a room full of people, all in touch with their sadness, disappointments and perplexity. I said to myself, "You have really goofed because you don't know the answers to these peoples' needs." At that point, two people entered the worship place carrying a jug of wine and a loaf of bread and we were invited to the Lord's Table.

I realized that my sense of value and worth did not depend on the success or failure of Faith at Work, but upon my relation with the crucified and risen Christ. That experience gave me new energy and hope and confidence and a sense of self-worth, and the circumstances of my situation were no longer controlling me and crushing me. Life felt like it was under control again. So there is a sense in which life in close relationship to God is a life of control and it feels very good and for some maybe very victorious.

Life continued to be very ambiguous, but I was not being tossed around by the circumstances because, if I may say, the focus for me had changed from my circumstances to my relationship with Christ. However I must not fall into the trap of thinking that if I am committed to Christ, life will no longer be ambiguous. The point is that whether I am in relation to God or not, life is ambiguous, but being in a conscious relationship with Christ enables me to cope with the ambiguities in a way that I cannot when I am not in a meaningful relationship with God in Christ.

The truth is that we don't like ambiguity and uncertainty. I don't like it. I was "shaped" not to like it. I was taught that life is something to be tamed and controlled. Isn't that what pension plans, RRSP's, annuities, investments, medical plans, etc., are all about? Because we don't like uncertainty, many of us have been willing to accept other peoples' answers about the questions of life, rather than embrace the uncertainties. Just listen to the radio and television preachers. They preach with absolute certainty. Every issue is clearly black and white ... right or wrong. It is a very seductive message. Unfortunately, it is not true.

One year in California, I did a workshop entitled, "A Faith that Works." Because of the subject matter, the workshop drew a large response. About half way through the workshop, I became aware that the participants and I had two different ideas about a faith that works. They wanted me to tell them something they thought they didn't know, but which I knew, that would make their faith work. It was as if they thought I had a secret about making a faith work, and they had come to hear me tell them the secret.

I, on the other hand, was trying to tell them that their faith journey, which was ambiguous and uncertain, was a journey of faith and it was working. I was saying, "Ambiguity is what faith is all about." I was trying to say to them that ambiguity and uncertainty are the context of faith. They are not an alien land. It is the homeland for people of faith. "Your faith is working, hang in there." I wanted them to know that the secret of a faith that works is that there is no secret. But they did not want to hear that. They were looking for something to clear up the uncertainties of life. They wanted to know the secret.

When you think of the people of Israel in Egypt, my guess is that most of us have some very negative images of their experience. Words that come to mind might be death, darkness, slavery, oppression, bricks and straw and those were certainly part of their experience. But what about Egypt as a place of refuge and provision for the people of Israel?

Read Genesis 47 where we are told, "Send me your fathers and your brothers in the best of the land." In verse 12, "And Joseph provided his father, his brothers and all of his father's household with food according to the number of their dependents." In verse 27, "Thus Israel dwells in the land of Egypt, in the land of Goshen and they gained possessions in it, and they were fruitful and multiplied exceedingly."

The point is that the journey of the Children of Israel was never just one thing. It was never unambiguous. And that is true of my faith journey. It has never been unambiguous. Parts of it have been warm and comforting, inspiring and hopeful. Other parts have been painful, inexplicable and dark.

The good news for Israel is that for 400 years, they were blessed in Egypt. They lived in the grasslands of Goshen. They had plenty of water, good soil, crops and the refinements of life. They multiplied and they prospered. The bad news was that a new king, who knew nothing of the arrangements between his predecessors and the people of Israel, came to power. He saw Israel as both useful and dangerous. Only the intervention of God and the leadership of Moses allowed them to make their escape.

But you can see the ambiguous quality of life even in their escape. You would think that getting out of Egypt would be good news and the most important thing in the lives of the Israelites. However, as difficult as it was to get the Israelites out of Egypt, it was equally difficult to get Egypt out of the Israelites. When things got difficult in the wilderness, they looked back. So deliverance was more difficult than Moses, and perhaps even Jahweh, anticipated.

I identify with the people of Israel because when things were going badly for me in my job in the States, I can remember "looking back" so to speak and thinking that maybe the quiet and predictable waters of Ontario hadn't been so bad after all. And I complained to God saying, "Why have you brought me here? It would have been better to have let me die at home, rather than in this strange land." You see, in the stress, I had forgotten that I had made the decision to move to the United States.

So when we are confessing Jesus Christ as the light of the world, we are not, I believe, inviting people to some form of triumphant, victorious living. We are not suggesting that they move from black to white. We are not suggesting that life under Christ is unambiguous. But by our confession of Jesus Christ as the light of the world and the Lord of our lives, we are declaring that life in Christ enables us to face the ambiguities of living with hope and with courage.

To tell people that the Christian life is one of victorious Christian living is to set people up. Their life experience will not support or sustain it, nor will the scriptures.

---

**Your immediate gut-level reaction to this chapter.**

**Your reflected response after two or three days.**

**Any differences between your reaction and reflection? Is there anything you need to do?**

## Chapter 5

*The Garment Bag*

# The Anachronism of the Professional Ministry

The following story will appear in the *The Halifax Globe and Leader Post* on November 15th, 1998:

At the next General Council of The United Church of Canada, which will coincide with the beginning of the twenty-first century, a dramatic change will be introduced, said the General Secretary, because of the continuing decline in membership.

From 1967 to 1987, membership in the United Church dropped by a startling 250,000. The loss continues, so that by the year 2000, an additional 150,000 persons, it is projected, will have left. This escalating loss of members has seriously affected the church's ability to continue with any kind of new church development. Overseas programs are soon to be closed out and the Pension Fund is in serious difficulty and is expected to be exhausted within four years. It is also anticipated that all thirteen Conference Offices which presently cost The United Church of Canada something over $4 million will be closed.

Although the General Council offices moved to Guelph, Ontario in 1994 to combat the rising costs in Toronto, and staff at the General Council has been cut by a whopping 43 percent, it has not been sufficient, says the General Secretary, to compensate for the loss of revenue from the membership of the church to the M&S Fund, from which overseas work, pensions, etc. are funded.

A reliable source indicated that it is the congregations in the city that are most seriously affected by the loss of members and revenue. The urban churches are quickly becoming a thing of the past and are closing at the rate of one every two months. Suburban churches are also in great difficulty. Only a few are still able to maintain a minister and staff. Others are seeking to prolong their work by amalgamation with other congregations. The projections for the next 20 years indicate an even greater decline and result in the General Council's dramatic proposal.

At the 38th General Council in the year 2000, the General Council of The United Church of Canada will propose that beginning in the year 2005, there will no longer be a paid professional ministry supported by a local congregation or the church at large. Although the church will continue to prepare men and women for leadership and perhaps even ordination/commissioning, though that has not been finally decided, the church will only choose candidates from among those who have already prepared themselves for another profession or work. The clergy of the twenty-first century will be required to exercise a tent-making ministry. That is, all seminary trained church leaders will need to be fully employed in some work other than in the church, and will then give volunteer leadership to the new small congregations to which they have been called.

For many, this seems to be a return to the New Testament ministry of St. Paul, but it should be obvious, as one minister said, that the church is not taking this unprecedented step out of some sense of leading by the Holy Spirit. The bottom line is strictly economic.

The General Council is making this momentous proposal because it is convinced that the only hope for the church now is an active, committed and highly motivated laity, which is enabled for ministry by a new kind of clergy.

While there is no doubt in the church's corporate mind that the loss in membership will continue, it does not know and cannot predict what additional losses will result if the proposal concerning the professional ministry is carried. Although the General Council hopes there will be a strong support for their position by the general membership, it is not sure what percentage of the people will support the decision and respond to the challenge. "One thing is clear," said one veteran minister, "if it goes through, it won't seem like church anymore."

There is, as one might imagine, mixed reaction among the clergy. Some are very excited. They realize that this will mean a dramatic change in their role, status, and life-style, but they are hopeful about a new role that will focus on the laity and help them to discover, claim, and use their gifts.

Others are very pessimistic. They cannot conceive of the new ministerial role. They believe that men and women must continue to be "set aside" to lead the congregation. It is a full-time position, they say. They cannot imagine lay people doing what they, for so long, have been doing. What concerns the General Council Executive is that they cannot be sure of how many clergy will be willing to accept the new role and take the necessary enabling training.

The next five years promises to be the time of greatest uncertainty in the life of the United Church. Freda Forthright (chair of Middleduck Presbytery) and past moderator, Harold Angel, said that this action of the General Council may prove to be the biggest bungle in the history of the church, or the smartest, most biblical decision it has ever made. Only time will tell.

Does that seem like an impossible story? It does not to this writer. In fact, another 11 years of continuing the present form of Sunday worship, the lack of community and the church's general irrelevance to the lives of our people, may make even this proposal to the 38th General Council too late.

We must, among other things, get away from the idea that the life and well-being of the congregation depends upon a professional ordained/commissioned person. Every day that we continue with that mindset is a further denigration of the laity and the membership of the church.

The General Council of the United Church and other mainline denominations should immediately commission the setting up of new models of congregational life based, for example, on the model of the community church in Columbia, Maryland of which we spoke earlier or other models that demonstrate that the treasure is in the people.

The reason why the congregation in Columbia is important is because it took seriously not only the new role of clergy, but also the role of the laity in whom our future rests. The minister in that congregation was called the Enabling Minister. He had a new and exciting leadership role which was to encourage the laity in the realization that they are gifted and to help them discover those gifts and encourage the people in the use of their giftedness. The laity was taken seriously in terms of expectations. If you wanted to go beyond being merely a Sunday worshipper and to become a member of the congregation, certain things had to be done.

First of all you had to write the Council and ask to become an intern and state your reasons. Then you must be a part of the Worship Committee from time to time. You must take the five or six courses being offered by the congregation in New Testament, Old Testament, Ethics, Personal Faith, etc.

You would be a part of one of the mission groups. A word should be said about these mission groups. Unlike the groups in most of our churches, which are there by reason of some Manual provision or some hierarchical decision, the mission groups in the community church in Columbia were there because of a sense of inner call. For example, if someone felt strongly about the peace issue, they would discuss it with the church council. If the council felt it was indeed a genuine sense of call, they would invite that person to speak about it at a Sunday service and to invite others who had a similar concern to join that person after the service with a view to commencing a new mission group.

The mission group might last six months or six years, it didn't matter. But what you had was a group of people coming together because they wanted to be there and because they wanted to do something. No one was there simply representing some other group or because they happened to be the chair of some other committee in the church. The mission group would meet every week, do the lectionary Bible study that all of the groups were doing and which was the basis of the Sunday morning worship, and then focus on their particular area of concern.

So if you wanted to become a member of the church you had to join one of the existing mission groups. And finally, you are asked to tithe 10 percent of your gross income. We need to remember that all of the above is subject to all the pain, misunderstanding, sin and self-centeredness of the people involved. In other words, I am not describing "perfection."

My secretary, in typing this manuscript, asked me in a rather pointed way, "Was this church in Columbia perfect? I've never heard you say anything negative about it." Well of course it wasn't perfect and never will be. In fact, what made it so attractive and effective for me was the imperfection of the members of the community. Earlier I described the members and adherents as mostly divorced or separated form their spouses. That was and is an accurate and important fact. It was their openness and vulnerability about the brokenness (imperfection) in their lives that created the unique environment and community. They were obviously and patently more imperfect than any group or church I have ever experienced. They were not fundamentally different from other church groups, but they differed in their openness about their needs and failures and pain and hopes and that in turn helped to develop an environment that enabled a process of new clergy roles and lay leadership.

So often in our churches today members are put in an either/or situation. They are either committed to evangelism or to social action, to personal congregational growth or to mission outside the local congregation. But here in this community church the personal faith journey and the reaching beyond self and the congregation went together as naturally as tennis and hot showers, or Rogers & Hammerstein, or Gretzky and hockey.

Of course, the corollary to the setting up of new models of congregational life in order to take seriously the clergy and the laity is that we are not now taking seriously our ordained/commissioned persons or the general membership in ways that are appropriate for the times in which we live. Maybe the format of a professional ministry set aside for the work of ministry was appropriate at one time in the life of the church. Maybe sitting people in rows to listen passively was right at one time. But neither of these are appropriate any longer.

The possibility of the institutional church seeking new models of congregational life is not without some hope. In November of 1988, the New Ministry Council of Halton Presbytery, Hamilton Conference, asked my wife and I to come and tell them about the experience we had in Columbia, Maryland. After an hour, we expected the Council to thank us appropriately and say that they would consider it. Instead, a motion was immediately passed saying that they would go to the Presbytery and inform the Presbytery that they had instructed us to attempt to set up an alternate congregational model.

After doing all the politically correct things, such as meeting with clergy and laity and writing letters to explain what was happening, we announced a meeting for those who were interested in doing church differently. A dozen men and women showed up. We explained what we were about and at the first meeting they agreed that at the end of eight or nine weeks we would assess how it was going.

The Thursday night meetings were mostly community building and doing a kind of relational Bible study. Attendance varied, but was usually five to six. At the end of nine weeks, we determined that while the people coming found it helpful, they had no intention or desire to leave their own present congregations in order to do church differently. What we were doing was interesting and helpful and supplemented their regular church life. What we were really looking for were people for whom the usual Sunday service and church life were not agreeable or helpful but who still wanted to be part of a community of faith. We later placed ads in local newspapers and advertised the idea of doing church differently but there was no response. Although this experiment did not work out, it did demonstrate that there are persons of vision and concern within the structures of the church and that should give us some hope.

It is also encouraging that Waterloo Presbytery of Hamilton Conference has undertaken an experiment of doing presbytery differently in order to bring new life, energy, and fellowship to the life of the presbytery. It is modelled on an experiment of a presbytery of the Presbyterian Church, (USA) in California. David Suzuki says that we have 10 years left to change our lifestyle in order to save the environment. I am suggesting that we have about ten years to change the way in which we are doing church or we shall be reduced to an historical memory. It is not just because of the boredom of Sunday morning or the irrelevancy of church life or the lack of community but also because of the age of the people in our churches. That fact surrounds everything with a sense of urgency.

Because of my availability in the Conference Office, I am asked to take part in a large number of anniversary services. What I notice first about the congregations is that nine out of ten of them are made up of men and women my age (64) or older. That is very frightening because in 10 to 15 years most of them are going to be joining me in some retirement-nursing home. They are not exactly excited by or energized by the thought of radical change. Someone must enable them, as well as younger members of the congregation, to see that the situation must change because times are critical.

In his book, *Liberation Theology*, Phillip Berryman speaks of the Reformation and says that Luther and others were not talking about abstract ideas, but in reality were concerned about new kinds of congregations and new kinds of leadership. That is what is required today: a re-examination of our congregational life and leadership, so that we may once again regain our energy and excitement about the work of the church.

Daniel Berrigan speaks for us today when he says, "Today we stand on the brink of the unknown; which is to say: things are normal and good, and permissive of joy."

---

**Your immediate gut-level reaction to this chapter.**


**Your reflected response after two or three days.**


**Any differences between your reaction and reflection? Is there anything you need to do?**

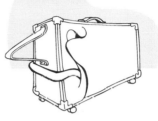

## Chapter 6

*The Pullman*

# The "Second Bestness" of an Achievement-Centred Life

W hen my father retired after a successful career, he felt he was a failure. Sometimes I feel the same way. I get to thinking I haven't done much of importance. No one will remember me for anything I have contributed. I haven't achieved very much. It has all been rather a waste of time. But recently, something has helped me to see things a little differently.

After I resigned from Faith at Work, I had no place to go and no job in sight. I saw an ad for a Professional Development in Ministry course at a seminary that would, it said, help me to discover my gifts and talents. Well, that seemed very timely. Perhaps if I took a course, it or they or someone could tell me what I should do next, so I enrolled.

A few weeks later, I received four booklets that I was to complete before the course. One booklet was entitled, *An Analysis of Meaningful/Effective Ability*. Step one in the book was to brainstorm about the significant processes, achievements and failures in my life. The book said that I might have difficulties in distinguishing between processes and achievements, and I did. But, as I studied the examples, I realized that while the processes might be related to the achievements, they were significant solely for the doing of them, not for the end results. Do you get that? A significant process is something of a continuing nature, whereas a significant achievement is something you succeed in finishing. With achievement, the end result is a major part of the significance. For the process, it is not.

I realized that how I measure success will determine how I feel about myself. If I measure my sense of worth and value based on my achievements, I might be in trouble. In fact, I know I would. But if I measure success on some really significant processes, I would do a lot better.

Once I clarified process and achievement, I was, according to the instructions, supposed to write out as many significant processes as I could think of. As you know, when you are describing processes, you usually use words ending in "ing" which indicate an on-goingness about the circumstances. For example, I put down "serving in the Navy, attending law school, deciding to go to seminary, being married, raising children, etc." Then I was to do the same thing for achievements. Here the operative words often end in "ed" or words that indicate an end. For example, "commissioned at 19, finished law school, graduated from seminary, invited to join Faith at Work, etc."

Failures, the instructions said, unlike processes or achievements, are more evaluative. The authors of the booklet were not interested in minor disappointments, but with major events in which you felt that you had failed in your objectives. While not everyone feels that there are significant failures in their lives, I thought of three.

The next step was really significant for me. I was to look over all three lists and pick out the nine which were the most significant and write a short description of each. When I finished, I made a rather important discovery. Seven of the nine which I had chosen were "processes." Do you see what I am saying?

Seven of the nine of the most significant experiences in my life were processes, not achievements. In other words, the exercise showed me how important process is to me, but I had been putting myself down because I thought I had not achieved much. If process is the criteria for measuring success, I could give myself at least an "A+."

To graduate from seminary was important; without a piece of paper I could not be ordained. But the "process" of the three years was more important. If I had focused solely on the fact of graduation, I would have missed the process which included the relationships with students and teachers and family.

Being asked to be president of Faith at Work was an achievement, but "being" president was far more important. It was in the being that I discovered that life was difficult. It was in the process that I cried, despaired, and felt sorry for myself. It was in the process that I found out my real value and worth did not depend upon the success of Faith at Work, but upon my relationship to Jesus. It was in the process that I became aware that I had nothing more to offer Faith at Work, and it was time to quit. For me, achievement had a lot of ego needs written all over it. The process is a learning place, a risking place, and a hopeful place.

To say we raised five children is an achievement, of course. But "raising" five children is something else. It is the raising that is full of memories. It is the raising that brings joy and pain, hope and disappointment, love and respect, forgiveness and acceptance.

Achievements are goal-centered, and they are important. Processes are people-centered, and they are primary. Right now, I feel like crying, because I realize that so much of my life has been achievement-centered, in order to be recognized. It is only now, when I take time to be quiet, to think and get in touch with myself, that I know that it is the process that really counts.

I enjoyed being a pastor, but I wanted to be a great preacher. Starting the first telephone ministry in Canada, using trained lay people, was terribly important, but I wanted to be recognized for doing it. In Faith at Work, we always said that it doesn't matter who gets the credit for what we do, as long as it is done. In a way, that is true, but in another way, I wanted my own denomination to say, "You've done a great job." When I didn't receive much recognition for what I had done, I quickly judged myself as a failure and missed the most important part — the process. It is the process that really counts, even if I keep messing that up.

How easily I can forget. Just a few months before I left Faith at Work, when I was telling the Administrative Committee of the Board that I was feeling very ambivalent about my future with Faith at Work, a Board member asked me, "Do you feel that your five years with Faith at Work has been successful?" I replied, "I don't think so." Do you know why I said that? Because I was once again measuring success by achievement. Faith at Work, under my leadership, had not been restored to its former place of importance in the Christian community, and so I felt that I had failed. When I stop that kind of personal put-down, I see that the process is what really counts.

Jesus said, "Come follow me" to several people. It occurs to me as I am writing this that these were not only invitations to do something, but also invitations to enter into a process with Jesus. I am sure that if you asked the disciples to make a list of their most significant achievements, one would be the decision to follow Jesus. But it was in the process of following Jesus that they discovered the promises of God, the fulfillment of their hopes, and the reality of sin, death, denial, and hope. Achievement has a terminal point in time. Process goes on. When I accepted Jesus into my life, that was an important day on my calendar, but it has been the process of following Jesus for over 30 years that has brought life and hope. For me, it is the process that counts. I hope I can remember that!

The reason I belabour the point is because we in the church have tended to emphasize achievement and we do that because we are reflecting contemporary society which focuses on achievement. Over and over again, I have heard clergy say that building churches is a sure way to get people involved and excited. And it makes sense. They have a goal and it is clear. They know what they can do. Others have said to me that a mortgage is a must because it keeps a congregation motivated toward a definite goal which they can achieve. But the down side is that when the building is complete or the mortgage paid off, many of those who were deeply involved leave, because achievement is the goal and there is nothing else to do.

With our focus on achievement such as stewardship, large congregations, visitation plans, local budgets, music, and preaching, we are robbing our people of the best part which is the process.

A lot of our people don't have a great sense of achievement or accomplishment in the church, although some take vicarious pride in the fact that they belong to a church which is the largest in Canada, where the preaching is the best or they have sponsored the largest number of candidates for the ministry. Spiritually they tend to think that others are better than they are, especially the clergy. But if we were to ask our people to pick out the really significant experiences in their lives, my guess is that they would mostly pick processes for which they could give themselves an "A+" rather than a failing grade. Achievements are important, but processes are people-centered and they are primary for us in the church.

This is simply another illustration of what was said in the first chapter on the importance of our history and telling our story. The biblical story which is our gospel is a process. Our experiential theology is a process and it is in the sharing of that, that we encourage one another. Our achievements tend to be threatening. However, sharing our process is affirming and bridge-building and therefore is an integral part of community building which is central to our well-being as a church and as congregations.

---

**Your immediate-gut level reaction to this chapter.**

**Your reflected response after two or three days.**

**Any differences between your reaction and reflection? Is there anything you need to do?**

## Chapter 7

*The Shoulder Tote*

# The Bondage of a Past Vision

Recently a member of a political panel on a program broadcast by the CBC, said that Sir John A. MacDonald had a vision for Canada from sea to sea and from east to west, but that that vision was no longer appropriate.

What is true of Sir John's vision for Canada, is, I submit, equally true of the vision for the new United Church of Canada in 1925. The Basis of Union says, "It shall be the policy of the United Church to foster the spirit of unity in the hope that this sentiment of unity may in due time, so far as Canada is concerned, take shape in a Church which may fittingly be described as national." Big is better! That vision, exciting as it may have been, is no longer a vision which is "in synch" with the times. A big national church today is anathema.

It is strange that 65 years after the birth of what many hoped would develop into a national church, there should be such a strong congregational emphasis and much distrust of the General Council, which is the symbol of a national church from east to west. There are few at this time who would rally around the vision of a national and uniting church. The fact is, today there is no vision for the church at large. What is developing, however, are strategies for survival. Indeed, we are living in a time of few visions anywhere. It is difficult to catch or see a vision when you are retreating. And the church is retreating at an ever-accelerating pace. We are lucky if we can articulate a vision for a local congregation, let alone for the church-at-large. It is doubtful if even Gunga Din and his bugle could help us at this point.

The church today is not unlike the Province of Quebec. It is looking for an identity, but the rest of the community, like the attitude of many Anglophones toward Quebec, could not care less.

Let me suggest to you what the next 10 years might look like if we fail to find a vision appropriate for our time or even if we do find a vision. Within the next decade, our identity, our vision of who we are or have been as a church, will be shaken as never before. Our reason for being will be severely challenged. The question of inter-faith relations will make the homosexual issue seem like a Sunday school picnic. If the ordination issue touched a raw nerve, the inter-faith issue will traumatize the Body. And we cannot avoid it. Indeed the United Church is promoting the moment of inevitable conflict, though that is not its intention. A special edition issue of the United Church's *Mandate* entitled, "Canada's Cultural Mosaic," carried articles by Clifford Hospital, Principal of Queen's Theological College and John Berthrong, former Inter-faith Dialogue Secretary of the Division of World Outreach of the United Church, in which the authors offer a position of accommodation to other faiths, but say nothing about the problem of exclusivity concerning Jesus Christ that the church has traditionally proclaimed and which has and will cause inter-faith conflict.

In the report of the Division of World Outreach to the General Council (Record of Proceedings, 32nd General Council, pp. 605 - 607) it is stated that the Division helps to plan and execute inter-faith programs internationally, nationally and locally. The Inter-faith Committee of the Division of World Outreach has recommended that inter-faith dialogue needs to become more grounded in the life of United Church people and congregations and we realize what that will do to the church's sense of identity.

The report also praises the new inter-faith Vision Television because it expresses the Canadian hope that we could all co-operate together in creating a harmonious pluralistic society with space for everyone. The day is coming when the "other faiths" will demand a serious and no-holds-barred discussion on the relation of Christianity to "other faiths." These "other faiths" are going to take seriously the vision of the Division of World Outreach, that there is space for everyone, but with the added word "equal." "Equal" space for everyone and equal in this context means pari passu — without preference.

The recent decision of the Ontario Supreme Court (January 31, 1990) which declared that any Ontario Public School religious course aiming indoctrinate students in any one faith is "illegal," is another clear indicator of the confrontation to come.

We can no longer continue our conversations with "other faiths" from the lofty position of John 3:16: "God loved the world so much that he gave his only Son, that everyone who has faith in him may not die but have eternal life." We can no longer dialogue from a position of those who hold the "truth." The exclusive factor of Christianity meaning that Jesus Christ is the incarnation, will be challenged as never before.

What can we expect? These people whom we have sought to convert and proselytize have now moved next door in a literal sense. They have immigrated to Canada. They have become our neighbours and we have found them to be people of grace, integrity and discipline. They have built their temples and mosques and when their numbers are sufficient to risk confrontation, they will. They will demand that the church talk to them as equals, each of whom has a right, but different, view of God.

At that moment, the mainline Protestant churches will split into those who accept the position that Christianity is only one of several living religions and those who will believe, like the people of Israel, that they are the chosen people of God in the midst of false gods and prophets. It may be of some comfort to know that as we in the United Church proceed into our wilderness, we will be accompanied by the Presbyterians, the Anglicans and other Protestant mainliners.

The "people of Israel" group will probably join with the Pentecostals et al. This will be followed by one final union for The United Church of Canada. The Anglicans, smaller in number, will come to the United Church people asking for a union, in the hope that such a union will increase the chances of survival. This time, the Anglicans will not require the re-ordination of United Church clergy, and the United Church, in a delightful act of non-revenge, will be willing to recognize the clergy of the Anglican church. But the Anglican Primate will not be number one in the new denomination. A larger, but fundamentally lifeless denomination, will have been created. In the end, the Presbyterians, predictably, will prefer to die alone, even though they are now preparing to give themselves corporate C.P.R.

Every week, I hear people in the church say, "We need a vision." You've heard it too! I would like a vision. Twice in my life, I have been part of ministries that had visions (Telecare and Faith at Work) and they were energizing and gave me and others something to believe in and work for. I think that we are all looking for a vision or a dream, something to believe in, because the payoff is so desirable.

But this is not a time for visions or dreams, in the sense of the future. It is a time to fulfil the "dream of becoming." It is pay-up time. It's demonstration time. It is a time to stop avoiding the reality of the present by focusing on the future. One of the realities of the present is the scandal of how we have been treating one another in the United Church this past year. And my guess would be that it is no different in other denominations. It's just that the issue of the ordination of practicing homosexual persons brought reality to the surface. The membership in the United Church has become an offence to the dream of St. Paul which is described for us in I Corinthians 12. Men and women left the United Church this past year over the issue of the possible ordination of self-declared practicing homosexuals. But a greater reason for leaving the church then and now in my opinion, is the way in which people in the United Church have treated one another.

In November, 1989, when representatives from the Community of Concern and the Executive of General Council were finally ready to sit down and talk for the first time after eight months of accusing, blaming and slandering one another through the media, the Executive of Hamilton Conference wrote to the Community of Concern and the General Council asking for a new climate in which to talk about the differences. The letter said:

> We are writing to you as representatives and spokespersons of the General Council and the Community of Concern.
>
> We believe that the decision of the General Council is still the divisive issue, but the manner in which we are dealing with our differences is, in our opinion, scandalous.
>
> So far we have failed to listen to each other, consulted our lawyers, discussed the issue in the media, threatened to leave or withhold our money, made bureaucratic responses, pretended there was no problem, voted no confidence in our leadership, threatened to sue for our property, slandered one another, threatened to discipline, created a new denomination, and we have in various other ways steamed, puffed and strutted.
>
> We believe that the reason we are experiencing so much pain is because few of us really believe 1 Corinthians 12. Few seem to believe that those on the opposite side can be inspired by the same Holy Spirit. Right now, both sides of the issue seem to be dismissing one another, on the basis that the Holy Spirit is more on their side than the other.
>
> When your respective "teams" sit down for dialogue, we urge them on behalf of the whole church, to first:
> 1. Confess our arrogance and down-putting of one another;
> 2. Ask for forgiveness on behalf of all of us;
> 3. Affirm one another as brothers and sisters in Christ;
> 4. Then ask what does this mean to the way that we should seek understanding and resolution of our differences.

We now know that none of that happened. Such expectations may have been premature.

It is interesting that in Joel 2:23-30, it was after the people of Israel repented (which is another way of dealing with the present garbage) and began to give thanks to God for their salvation and all the goodness that had come to them, that they then, by the Spirit, began to have dreams, visions and prophesy about the Kingdom of God.

I believe that today, we are in a Joel 2 church. We need to repent for our unwillingness to take seriously 1 Corinthians 12, which was Paul's dream for the integrity of the church. Just how a group of people such as the "People of Israel" or the United Church corporately repents is not clear to me.

Paul knew that people in the church could and would have different views and interpretations. He knew that they would lust after their particular views, but he dreamed of a Gospel that would enable people to be accepting of one another, that would enable men and women to believe in and affirm the commitment and integrity of others. That is why he used the image of a body. What is there that is so integrated as the human Body? What is there that is so inter-dependent? If the body parts don't recognize their intimate connections; if they don't care for each other; if they don't realize that they are an ecology of suffering and rejoicing, then it won't work, it won't be believable, it will have no integrity.

Well the analogy is obvious. Today the body called the church is increasingly losing its credibility because we don't take seriously 1 Corinthians 12. It is yet another part of the Bible that is not authoritative in our lives. Of course, the Protestant church is a scandal of bodily indifference. There are thousands of examples of various parts of the body claiming to be more important, more correct and able to live without other parts.

This past year has demonstrated beyond question that the sin of "body-parts pride" continues. Parts of the body known as the United Church are claiming that they can separate and still be whole. Other parts remain, claiming that their interpretation of the bodily parts are more correct than other interpretations. Maybe St. Paul was just a dreamer after all. Maybe the church, as the Body of Christ, is really only the church invisible. Maybe it's true that we are not one in the spirit.

I, for one, have to believe in Paul's dream of bodily integrity because I fell for the party line which said that when I became a Christian, things would be different. I would be different, a community called the church would be different, so I have to believe that treating one another differently than the world, is not only a possibility, but our mandate. The reason it is important now, perhaps more than ever before, is because to avoid it is a cop-out. It always was a cop-out, but today it seems more critical. It is easier to hold talks about theology and positions and how things used to be, than to sit down and talk honestly about why we cannot get along with brothers and sisters in Christ. And the last five words are crucial. We are not talking about conversations between good and bad people, or between believers and non-believers, but rather conversations between believers, each of whom thinks that they are right.

It is this belief in one's position that is causing such stress, polarization, pain and broken relationships. Yet all this is acceptable to some, because of the desired goal of certitude. More than that, the battle for certitude is acceptable in spite of the casualties because it is believed by the respective sides that what is being done by their side is sanctioned by God and the Bible. They each honestly believe that the position they seek to establish is what God wants. It is the Crusades all over again, only this time the victims are not the infidels, but brothers and sisters in Christ.

Such a way may be appropriate for some denominations, but it is not right for The United Church of Canada. Our history is one of being inclusive, not exclusive. That's who we are in the United Church. The dream of 1925 was that of uniting persons of different Christian experience and tradition. That dream has served us well for 65 years. It has been a tradition of generous spirit, which has allowed for a wide latitude of opinion and practice in what we call "essential agreement."

But now in the 1990's, the stress and strife, the challenges and changes, seem to have reached an unacceptable crescendo. We seem, according to some, to be under attack at every level. Political systems are under attack. There is terrorism, war and threats of war. Marriage and family values seem to be undermined in a multitude of ways. Conflict is arising as to whose values are right or should prevail within the church. There are struggles for the rights of homosexuals and the uncertainty about the rights of the fetus. No part of our lives seems to be secure these days from challenge and threat. It is no wonder that people want to find stability and solid ground somewhere.

It is therefore not surprising that people might look for that place of security and comfort in the church. And what happens as we seek a place of safe keeping and certainty and tranquility in the church? We begin to draw lines on people with whom we disagree. And when we do that, in the church, we begin to judge who is acceptable and who is not.

In my third year at Emmanuel College, there were 28 men who ranged in theological position from very conservative to ultra-liberals. One of the great advantages of being 35 when you graduate is that you know who is "in and who is not," "who is right and who is wrong," theologically speaking. So I drew some pretty clear lines on who was acceptable and a real Christian. Some 15 years later, I met one of those whom I had judged to be "out," on a plane to Chicago. For an hour and a half we had a Jerusalem Conversation at 35,000 feet. To my shame, I discovered that I was probably closer to him in my thinking and experience than anyone else I knew. But because I had drawn "lines" on him, I never took the time to know him or care about him and so held him at arm's length for 15 years. God forgive me! The problem is that while the line drawing is done under the name of God, or the Bible, the real motive, I suggest, is fear. The consequence is more distress within the church because of the polarization caused by people deciding who is "right" and who is "wrong" and who is "in" and who is "out."

We feel we must take charge. Culturally speaking, people in the church realize that they cannot take control. But there is one place that we can and that is in our own bailiwick - the church. Here in the church, we can begin to take charge and so we do by making statements, preparing position papers, demanding the resignation of those who don't behave as we deem they should. We affirm what we perceive to have been previously held Christian positions and in so doing, we feel good.

I had a former boss who was vice-president of one of the largest stockbrokers in New York City. After a certain period of success in climbing the corporate ladder, he received a "promotion" that turned out to be more lateral than vertical. He suddenly realized that he was out of control. His destiny with the company was in the hands of others. In the midst of all of the uncertainty surrounding him, he began to take off weight and he looked better than he had for 20 years. When I asked him about it, he said the feeling of being out of control at the job was overwhelming. He said, "I had to take charge somewhere. I had to get control somewhere and I discovered I could do that with my own body, so I did."

That seems to be what has happened in the church today. Those who are so uncomfortable because of the uncertain times in which we are living and who realize that they can't do much to change the culture in which we are living, have discovered that there is one place they can exercise some control and that is in the church and it makes them feel good. There is no vision in such courses of action based on fear or anxiety or anger or loss of revenue.

At the November 1989 meeting of the General Council Executive a four-year strategic proposal was printed in the workbook, but was not debated or acted upon. Now in fairness to the sponsors, I am sure the proposal was offered to help the church through the difficult years ahead. In the background material to the proposal (page GC76 f), the statement is made that, "members of the United Church are in need of learning again to live with diversity without divisiveness as a special calling of God for these times." I believe that is true. But in the very next paragraph, it states, "differences can be and have been dysfunctional in the church. Thus it is important to discuss the acceptable range or spectrum of differences; beyond which a denominational fellowship would not be able to function."

That is a "drawing lines on people" question. It is not the question we should be asking. It is not a United Church question. The important question is, "What is driving us to even ask such a question?" What is pushing us to feel the need to draw lines on other people? The answer, I suggest to you, is fear. It is driven by a need for control. It is a power question. And most important, it is not our kind of question.

Henri Nouwen in an interview was asked, "What is the most important issue that people are struggling with today?" His response was, "Fear." We in the United Church today, I suggest, are surrounded, besieged and encircled by fear. Some fear the leadership of homosexual persons. Others fear being oppressed and unaccepted. Still others fear losing traditional values, or the leadership in the church, or control of the present system, or not following Jesus, or not being just and loving or losing our faith.

It is certainly true for me. I am afraid that violence may be taken by unmovable positions. I am afraid of radical change or what my friends will do. I am afraid of taking a position and cutting myself off from some long-time friends. I am afraid of being inadequate. I am afraid for the church.

Nouwen says that "Fear is always connected to something we want to hold on to." Therefore it seems to me that it is imperative for us to prepare some process by which those differing points of view would meet, not to talk about theological positions, but to share our fears and why we are afraid, so that out of that human experience, we might be sensitive to the appropriate strategy for this time.

Hiring experts in strategic planning as the Presbyterians have done is an attempt to take charge, get control, demonstrate power and competency. It is not dealing with the prior question of what is driving us and others to the struggle for power in which we have become engaged and which will end in the injury of many.

The United Church is an attempt to give visibility to the great dream of St. Paul which finds expression in 1 Corinthians 12, a part of which is translated by Leslie Brandt in this way: "The gifts of the spirit differ, and so do the people who possess them. The spirit, however, is One and the same, and this makes everyone of God's children of equal value and importance to God." I suggest that we need to trust that original vision of the uniting churches which allowed for a wide scope of interpretation and opinion with a resulting richness, rather than seeing such diversity as threatening. The diversity and its resulting creative tension is who we are in the United Church. It is rich, full of possibilities, full of challenge and uncertainty and surprises, but all of it is based on our trusting the Living God, whom we believe we have come to know through the person of Jesus Christ. That I believe is an important part of the vision for the nineties — 1 Corinthians 12 — that the diversity of the Body of Christ, *is* the Body of Christ.

For some, this concern for 1 Corinthians 12 sounds too introspective. What the church must do, they say, is demonstrate its concern for justice and peace and creation. Well of course we should be concerned about these issues. The United Church has always been on the forefront of the social Gospel. But let us not be fooled. Issues, no matter how important, can also be a means of avoidance and escape. It is a lot easier for the church to preach about justice and peace and environment in the world than to face the lack of justice and peace within the church which brings us back to the resolution of the conflict facing the church today.

In the September/October, 1989 issue of *Action Information*, a publication of the Alban Institute of Washington, D.C., there is an article on Christian ministry in a pluralistic society. The author tells us that people and organizations usually operate according to a paradigm or model that they believe reflects reality. Then the author cites the work of David Kanton, a sociologist/psychologist, who spent time observing real families in their daily lives.

Kanton came up with three models. "Most easily recognizable is the traditional paradigm with its goal of maintaining the glorious traditions of the past. Usually organized in a hierarchical fashion, the traditional paradigm seeks clear roles and assignments and has strong boundaries to mark the difference between who is in and who is out.

"The second model is that of the individualistic paradigm which is not only congregational in its polity, but very often liberal in its theology. Change is the spice of life and innovate and create are the chants of this paradigm. Somewhere in the middle is the negotiating paradigm, which seeks to mediate, interpret, and promote growth. Elements of hierarchy and individualism are present at different times and leadership roles are clear, but shared. Unity and diversity is often the motto of this group."

It is interesting that people in the United Church divided themselves into these three paradigms during the past year. And it is not a case of deciding which of these is right or wrong, good or bad, because each represents a position of reality for those who belong to the various groupings. The point is that understanding these different models of perceived reality enables people to work more effectively together and there is far less blaming.

And that is the point of 1 Corinthians 12. Paul is calling for the recognition of diversity. He is not asking people to abandon or change their paradigm or the place from which to best express reality. It is not a call to make judgements or to blame. It is a call to reality. It is a call to abandon self-righteousness, it is a call to believe that the spirit can and does work in diversity. It is a call to believe the spirit of God and not our particular position. There is no salvation in conservativism or liberalism or fundamentalism or middle roadism. But, the problem today is not just one of diversity or gifts or ministries or service, say opponents to the ordination of self-declared practicing homosexual persons. It is a matter of some people in the church who would lead us in a path that is morally wrong. A position that is contrary to scripture and that we cannot condone.

That is why the only way to approach our differences is for all to come to the table in the spirit of contrition and confession of one's own personal failure to be God's person. We need to hold some "no-fault" conversations. There is no one in any of the above paradigms who is not needing forgiveness. There is no one who comes to the table with clean hands, but we can so easily ignore that by focussing on what is perceived to be the flaws in other people's thinking and practice.

This is not an argument for the position that anything goes. Rather it is a position, which if taken seriously, would allow for a new and different climate in which to talk to each other. Let us come to the table with our common humanity. The issues divide us. Our theology separates us. But we do have a great deal in common in terms of our humanity and the struggle we have to live out our lives as Christians.

When it comes to living life, we are indeed brothers and sisters. We are sojourners together. We are all facing the same problems, the same temptations, the same disappointments, the same hopes and dreams. So let us meet each other at the point of our shared humanity and from there move to the matters that divide us. This is no panacea or guarantee. It is an approach which takes seriously the dream of 1 Corinthians 12 and the reality of our humanity. Who knows what surprises might result? Who knows what new dream or vision might be born?

---

**Your immediate gut-level reaction to this chapter.**

**Your reflected response after two or three days.**

**Any differences between your reaction and reflection? Is there anything you need to do?**

## Chapter 8

*The Sample Case*

# The Wrong Mirror

A s a preacher, it is tough to admit or confess that Sunday at eleven o'clock is a boring time. That is like Boris Becker or Chris Everett saying that tennis is boring. I mean, Sunday worship used to be the highlight, the Wimbledon of my week. It is even tougher to admit that Reginald Bibby's conclusions about the church are right and that he is writing about me. It is not just the church that is reflecting or mirroring contemporary culture; I am too and I need help.

Maybe the biggest problem or obstacle for me has been to realize that I am a cultural reflector. As a matter of fact, I didn't consciously realize it until just six years ago, at the age of 59. Imagine going through three quarters of your life before realizing that you had been seduced by contemporary cultural values. But it's true! I did not personally realize that I had been captivated by the values of the world until December, 1984, when I went to Haiti to build houses under the auspices of Habitat for Humanity. Haiti, as many of you know, is considered to be the poorest and most poverty-ridden country in the western hemisphere.

Before I left, I read *National Geographic* with its full-colour pictures of the poor and the destitute. I knew about the struggle of the Third World countries. I could honestly say that I knew about these people ... in my head.

But *National Geographic* isn't filthy and dirty, it doesn't smell, it isn't covered everywhere with excrement. The glossy, full coloured pictures don't really communicate the reality, at least not to me. But living there did — in some measure.

After we arrived in Haiti, our first stop was the police station where in the fashion of a grade "B" movie, we walked through the wooden gates, guarded by a single soldier, and sat on three rows of wooden benches while the local gendarmes questioned us and noted our presence in Haiti as "house-building missionaries." Then we drove to the village of Dumay. It was only 15 miles from Port-au-Prince in the mountains, but it took us an hour to get there because of the "roads." They weren't really roads, just places where there were no trees. We settled into an unused medical clinic, consisting of two small rooms and a porch, along with a very hard concrete floor. Four of us "slept" — air mattress to air mattress in one room, three in the other, and three on the porch with the chickens and the rooster. (Did you know that roosters crow all night and not just at sunrise?) If it had not been for my double, high-powered sleeping pills, I think I would not have slept all week.

Since I am not a builder, I decided that I could do the least damage if I mixed cement. During the next week, my partner and I mixed what seemed to be about a million pounds of cement in a small wheelbarrow. The temperature was somewhere between 95 and 115 degrees Fahrenheit. By Wednesday, we would mix a little cement, then hide behind some cinder blocks to get some shade. Then mix some more cement. About a year later, the day was over and we would walk slowly home.

I have noticed that I am most "flip" when I am most anxious. I started off this trip scared. I guess it was because of the unknown. I was anxious about the primitive conditions that we were warned about, and I realized how addicted I am to the easy life. As the week moved on, I started making comments like, "I'll never criticize America again," or "I am going to sing 'God Bless America' and 'O Canada' every day in gratitude." In retrospect, I think it was my way of trying to distance myself from the situation. I also thought about buying a Mercedes-Benz when I got back. Maybe that would separate me from this awful and destructive filth, dirt, and poverty. After all the kidding and flippant comments, the bottom line for me was that no one should have to live in those conditions and certainly not me. I am not sure if I was angry at the situation in Haiti, or because of the cost to me to help change it, or because I didn't know what to do about it, or because the Haitians were everything I didn't want to be: powerless, poor, vulnerable, defenseless, dependent and fragile.

Going to Haiti was a painful experience and as much as I sometimes want to forget it, I hope I never can. I hope that I will never become unmindful of how some of God's people are having to live. But the real shock for me was the realization of what was number one in my life. In the context of that terrible poverty and filth, I realized that what was most important was not God or Christian values or serving the Church or all the other things I had been espousing, but my Canadian-American, comfortable, middle-class style of life. That is what was so threatened in Haiti, when I was confronted by that terrible vulnerability and poverty. I wanted to get back to the security of my middle class life-style with all of its comforts and controls and protection.

My guess is that if I had never gone to Haiti, I might never have discovered what was really most important to me. I would have gone on believing and thinking that God and Christian values were most important, while at the same time, living out the values of contemporary society and never "catching on" to the contradiction. I would have read Reginald Bibby's book, smiled and said, "Oh yes, I know some people like that."

The fact is that I never took Jesus or Paul seriously when they warned against the powers of this world. That sounded too spooky, too primitive, too unrealistic. Somewhere I got the crazy idea that as a Christian I was immune to the temptations of the world, because I didn't see these "powers" in the advertisements for cars and houses and clothes and success. I am not saying all these things are bad or evil. I am just saying that with their constant attractive presence, they can quite unconsciously become the norms and reasons for living. At least, that is what seemed to have happened to me.

Let's be clear! I am still a Christian. I am living proof that the victorious Christian life approach is not true. I am in a valley. I am struggling and I have to say to you that I believe it is okay to be where I am. I would not have chosen to be here, but it is not inappropriate for Christians to be in places of struggle. What is really tough is to be struggling and believe that it is not okay.

So what is the answer? I am not sure. But this is clear to me. Unless I find a community of believing strugglers, who share my concern and who by their corporate witness confirm the importance of doing something and holding me to it, I can't do anything. I just can't cope with the cultural powers by myself. In one of my many conversations with the Reverend Bill Fritz, of Barrie, Ontario, former chair of the Community of Concern, he spoke of the church as a "counter-culture" and I agreed that it should be. Without that kind of supportive, visible and accountable community, I cannot make it. Unfortunately, the church isn't that kind of counter-culture.

The immediate question would seem to be, "How do we become a counter-culture?" But there is a prior and more important question and by now, I am aware that we in the church aren't very good with prior questions.

Earlier we said that the prior question is not the interpretation of scripture, but whether the Bible is really authoritative. In Christian development the primary question is not producing programs, but to first discover where the people really are in their theology and faith. So with the matter of being cultural reflectors. The prior and primary issue is getting the laity and clergy in the United Church and others to admit that we are cultural reflectors. Then I have no doubt that we will begin to come up with some creative ideas.

It's that Joel 2 scenario again: when the people repented and began to give thanks, they began, through the Holy Spirit, to have dreams and visions about the Kingdom of God.

---

**Your immediate gut-level reaction to this chapter.**

**Your reflected response after two or three days.**

**Any differences between your reaction and reflection? Is there anything you need to do?**

## Chapter 9

*The Carry-On*

# The Peril of Riding Two Horses

I like Walt Disney movies. I like them because it is always clear as to who are the good guys and who are the bad ones. There is no ambiguity. It is black and white. It feels good to be so clear about the issues and the situations and people. But the real world isn't like that. The real world is ambiguous. The real world has few clear statements. In the real world there are no simple answers.

All of us live in the real world. Not only do we live in the real world, but we are part of the real world. We help create the ambiguity in the world. So why the demand for clear, unambiguous answers and statements concerning homosexuals at this time? I ask that, because all of us who are members of the church are so much a part of the ambiguity. We cannot separate ourselves from it. Moreover, I don't believe that we want to. We helped shape it. We support it and yet suddenly, in this issue of homosexuality, we hear demands for clarity, separation, distance, and certitude. People are asked to draw lines on what is acceptable and what is not.

On what basis do we do this? Don't misunderstand. I understand the desire for clarity about what is an appropriate life-style for those professing to be Christians. I need some definition of what practical, every-day,

Christian living looks like. We do need models. I know this sounds silly, but in the old days it was clear for some Christians at least, that one should not smoke, drink, neck, go to shows on Sunday, or dance. They should go to church every Sunday. That may sound crazy, given the life-styles of 1990, but right or wrong, those rules gave some direction and some parameters by which we could form judgements on how we should live and how we expected others to live.

But it seems that there are no such boundaries any more. I think there are no clear boundaries because we Christians, as well as the world, have blurred the definitions. Right or wrong, we knew a few years ago that divorce was wrong. Right! Jesus disapproved and divorced persons were given a hard time. But that guideline is very fuzzy today because so many marriages both in and out of the church end in divorce. So the church has accepted that reality. To try and save our position, some clergy insist on pre-marriage counselling for divorced persons because it is a way of expressing disapproval, while at the same time adding a little more gray to the scene.

The drinking of alcoholic beverages has always been a gray area. For United Church people the words of St. Paul once seemed to be important. That is, we are free to do anything, but not all things are a good idea. If what we are free to do causes a brother or sister to fall or stumble then we should refrain from that. So for years the United Church advocated total abstinence. Can you believe that? It's true. Today we say, "drink if you must, but be careful." What happened to our concern for the stumbling brothers and sisters? In any case, it added a great deal more gray to the situation. Of course the Anglicans have always grayed the question by their broad tolerance of social drinking.

When I was growing up a number of friends "signed the pledge." Now if you are under 50 years of age, you probably think that signing the pledge has to do with some sort of financial campaign. But that's not it. "Signing the pledge" meant promising never to drink alcoholic beverages. Like it or not, it gave some very clear definition to what was expected of a Christian. But you see, all these stimulating beer ads and attractive liquor ads and advertisements about wine with meals and the movies and TV have had their impact. They have converted a lot of old pledge-signers with the result that a large percentage of people in the United Church today now think it's alright to drink in some form or other. Ten years ago it would have been unthinkable for Christians to bring a bottle to a church conference or church meeting. Not today. The point is that by our own acceptance of the life-style of contemporary society concerning drinking, we have muddied the scene once again. The reality is that the majority of us in the church are contributing to one of the biggest drug operations in Canada and we think it's perfectly okay. That's gray, brothers and sisters!

And what about the permissive society? Now you're not going to suggest that church people have contributed to that are you, someone may ask? As a matter of fact, I am. I can't say for sure that church people watch the restricted movies or rent restricted videos, but I believe that we do. I can't say for sure that some people support violence and promiscuity, but I'll bet that we do by the "soaps" that we watch and the movies and videos that we rent without protest. Apart from the odd clergy person who preaches on the evils of contemporary movies, I have never heard any large group of church people raising their voices in protest. We tell our children that they shouldn't watch certain movies or videos and then we watch them ourselves. When it comes to this area folks, gray is definitely the predominant colour.

Do you know that the United Church at one time was really opposed to gambling? I know that's hard to believe. But it's true. J. R. Mutchmor, the one-time watch dog of our United Church morals, would turn over in his grave if he knew how many United Church people today and other Christians are buying lottery tickets. I can remember when I was growing up that the big deal was to buy an Irish Sweepstakes ticket once in a while which was against the law. But today, gambling is clearly a part of the contemporary society in which we are living and to which we Christians in large part contribute.

Just one more. In Acts 15 when the Jewish Christians wanted to lay the whole Judaic law on the new Gentile Christians, they held a meeting called the Jerusalem Council at which they decided not to burden the Gentiles with laws that they themselves could not keep. So they compromised and they said that all the Gentiles had to do was to abstain from things polluted by contact with idols, from fornication, from anything that had been strangled and from blood. Jesus also condemned the inappropriateness of fornication for Christians. But what has happened? Couples living together today before marriage is more the rule than the exception.

I don't know about you, but I haven't heard many of the churches say much about that because many of the children of the clergy and people in the church are involved in that kind of behaviour, and we parents can't decide whether we are mad or jealous. In a recent debate over the ordination of homosexuals the Community of Concern wanted to introduce a phrase about "fidelity in marriage and celibacy in singleness." But where did that come from? It didn't come as a protest against all of the fornicating that is going on among heterosexuals, but rather it was a way of reinforcing their protest against the ordination of self-declared practicing homosexuals. Let's face it. The church's silence on this issue has contributed a huge quantity of gray to living.

That's enough. What is the point? My point is, that we in the church have made a substantial contribution to the graying of our society and now we don't know what to do about it. It's out of control. The church really doesn't have much to say anymore that people will listen to because we no longer have clear lines about living. We have no clear alternatives.

Up until now, there has been no gut-level issue to galvanize our frustrations and guilt — not our passive acceptance of a permissive society, or our support of the provincial drug trade, or our gambling, or our lack of stewardship. But now there is!

The possibility of ordaining a self-declared practicing homosexual would be the ruination of our society they say. People feel so strongly about this issue that they have left the church and formed other groups. Others are threatening to leave if the United Church at its next General Council does not repudiate the present statement and make a clear unequivocal statement denouncing the ordination of self-declared practicing homosexuals.

Folks, I have just realized that this is nothing but scapegoating. Please note, I am not saying that homosexuality is right or wrong, or good or bad or what the origins are. Those are different issues about which the evidence is very ambiguous.

We in the church have surrendered on just about every other "moral" issue such as divorce, fornication, drinking, promiscuity, and stewardship. We are a reflection of contemporary society. We have been riding two horses. We are just a mirror and we feel terrible and afraid, but at last an issue has arisen on which we can demonstrate that we are different. Finally we can say "that's it," and that feels good.

In the midst of so much confusion by the experts and so much "gray painting" courtesy of contemporary society and the churches, how can we suddenly come out with clear, unambiguous statements? People have accused the United Church of producing an ambiguous document called "Membership Ministry and Human Sexuality," but I ask you how can we produce anything else given the society in which we live and which we in the church have helped to create?

The homosexuals are not the only scapegoats. Here's a partial list of others.

Order of Ministry persons are being scapegoated because certain laity are insisting that they are the role models of the church. In a sense we clergy are the authors of our own scapegoating. From the very beginning, when certain persons were set aside, we clergy accepted that special status with all its benefits. We allowed the spotlight to be upon us. We were after all, the ones "called," "set apart for special orders," "ordained." We were the shepherds and guardians of the faith. So it is not to be unexpected that people should focus on Order of Ministry people or today's commissioned persons as the role models. It's not that we should not be role models, but we can't carry all the baggage. After all, in the United Church, the laity outnumber the Order of Ministry persons by 200 to 1. What the emphasis on Order of Ministry people as role models does is provide an out for the laity. When it comes to role-modelling, the laity have copped out and are scapegoating the professional Christians if they don't measure up to their (laity) standards.

I don't know about you, but I have never heard about lay persons being disciplined by Sessions or presbyteries for sexual misbehaviour, or for income tax cheating, or too much drinking, or abusing wife and family. The laity, it seems to me, deal with their wrong behaviour vicariously through the Order of Ministry persons.

There are more scapegoats. Those who are in favour of the ordination of homosexual persons scapegoat the Community of Concern. "If they weren't around, all of our problems would be solved," they say. Others scapegoated the Moderator because he is a late-comer to Canada, doesn't speak English as well as his critics expect and because he is Korean. And then there is the General Secretary of the General Council and the staff of the General Council and Conference staff who are scapegoated by those opposed to the ordination of self-declared practicing homosexuals because they believe that these people are all in favour of the ordination and because they believe that they exercise too much influence in the Courts of the church.

At a recent course in conflict management, the instructor ventured the opinion that the homosexual issue in the United Church is only the presenting problem. That is to say, it is a real problem in its own right, but it is also the trigger that set off the explosion of many unresolved issues that have been smouldering for years in the United Church. When you talk to some of those who are most vociferous about "the issue" you often hear them say that this "issue" is the straw that broke the camel's back. What they are referring to is the unresolved conflict and anger over the New Curriculum of 25 years ago, the authority of scripture, the inclusive language problem, the United Church's view on abortion, the structures of the United Church and now the matter of the possible ordination of self-declared practicing homosexuals. And just as in a congregation, where anger has been stacking for years, it will finally explode. So today, the unresolved anger of the past 25 years has exploded in The United Church of Canada over the possibility of ordaining/commissioning self-declared practicing homosexuals.

The instructor in this conflict course felt that it was possible for a denomination to deal with all of its unresolved conflict if it chose. The point here is that it may be important for us to recognize the truth about the years of unresolved anger and address ourselves to some resolution of that, instead of being fooled into thinking that there is but one issue over ordination.

There is also a rather deliciously humorous quality in all of this. There have been a number of Order of Ministry persons who have left The United Church of Canada and a larger number of laity. Some have joined other churches or denominations. Others have created a new denomination. The ironic touch is that because many of them left the United Church before dealing with or processing their anger, they took it with them, and one day, just as sure as night follows day, all of that conflict and anger will erupt in the churches to which they have moved or established. Unfortunately, I don't expect to be around when it happens.

---

**Your immediate gut-level reaction to this chapter.**

**Your reflected response after two or three days.**

**Any differences between your reaction and reflection? Is there anything you need to do?**

## Chapter 10

*The Attaché Case*

# Dash to the Wire

In steeplechase racing, once you have cleared the last obstacle, it is a clear dash to the wire. That picture is not true of the Christian race. Even though we might change the way we do things, the possibility of new obstacles and old ways will continue to challenge us right down to the finish.

The point for me is that if we change the way we do things, it will enable us to face the new challenges and obstacles with greater confidence and strength. I say strength purposely, because the boredom of worship, the unreality of biblical authority, the expectancy of God to run our lives, the suppression of laity gifts, the weight of old visions and being a cultural reflector constitute a lot of heavy baggage. If they can be dumped, we can face the challenges and obstacles in our dash to the wire, with less encumbrances and more strength.

Let me rephrase that. Just think of how refreshed we would be in running the race set before us, if every Sunday the worship experience was genuinely life-giving, instead of life-draining. Imagine the enthusiasm, which is energy producing, that would result if we stopped trying to ride the twin horses of cultural and Christian values. A divided allegiance is very debilitating.

Taking charge of one's life is an empowering act. How liberated we would feel if we would unload the heavy burden of guilt we experience when we think that "struggling" is evidence of an inadequate Christian commitment.

Think of the healthy power that would be ours if we took seriously St. Paul when he says that all members of the Body are gifted. That means you and me. I cannot imagine how dynamic we would feel, if we allowed the experiences, the processes of our lives, to be the criteria of whether we are successful or not, rather than goal achievement.

I don't know about you, but I am tremendously invigorated by the possibilities of the future. But when my view of the future, when my attempt to discern the future is clouded and made foggy by old visions, it takes a lot of energy to cut through.

I have a sign in my office which says, "Do not give your heart to that which does not satisfy your heart." The reason why it is important to me is because to do so is very enervating. It wastes energy to give yourself to something which does not return energy and make you feel good.

And finally, painting the world gray with mixed messages leads to listlessness. That is not to say that we are to avoid ambiguity and uncertainty. We can't. But we can try to stop contributing to it. We should be painting the world with the bright colours of repentance and hope and newness and forgiveness and love and our humanness. Then, I suggest, we will be able to run to the wire with all its distractions and uncertainties with much confidence and a hope that transcends everything.

---

**Your immediate gut-level reaction to this chapter.**


**Your reflected response after two or three days.**


**Any differences between your reaction and reflection? Is there anything you need to do?**